# DON'T STOP ME NOW

MARCELLA SHERFY WALTER

Helena, Montana
2024

Cover photograph and design by Geoffrey Wyatt, Wyatt Design

ISBN: 9798330437658

*To honor the first believers:*
*Merle Ulery*
*Lee Lengel*
*Tom Govan*
*Bob Utley*
*Ivan and Carol Doig*
*Ron Brey and Claire Cantrell*

# TABLE OF CONTENTS

# INTRODUCTION

*I have a new tattoo.*

*The first time I posted blog essays and corralled them in a book, I called the whole enterprise Still Learning How to Fly. It's Rodney Crowell's rambunctious song, written in the shadow of a friend's looming death. All promise to live deeply for as long as fate permits. I had that title inked on my arm—a companion to Yes, Yes, Yes, Yes.*

*This year I added Don't Stop Me Now. Freddie Mercury's anthem when he was lead vocalist for the rock group Queen.\* Adam Lambert sings it now with incredible talent and panache as he headlines for Queen. So that title lives on my wrist along with some delicate art.*

*It's an ironic choice. I ended my earlier collection of essays sanguine about dying. My life had been so rich, so favored by the gods of friends and landscape and profession that I could go peaceably any time.*

*Still true. And still not the whole story. I've just gotten replacement knees. The more I hobbled around the more I wanted to walk. To see the Grand Canyon again and grandkids' basketball and baseball and art and just their journey to grown-up. I cannot imagine leaving the boys— the cats—or Birger Sandzen's backlit prints or my little alebrijes or the Big Belts or so many cocktail hours and phone calls and trips. There are so many more imagery-rich, heart-stopping books to read.*

*In the 1990s my cousin Gary (about whom I wrote) witnessed the horrors of his partner's death to AIDS. In those moments before effective medicine became available, Gary knew that he was likely to face similar agonies. On the one hand, he wanted to escape the suffering he'd seen. And on the other, he acknowledged that he—like his friends—might well sit up in the last moments, in the last misery and indignities and shout, "NO, not yet. Let me live a little longer."*

*Mostly, the timing of our death is not ours to choose. But the moments we are given allow us to witness the world's great sadness and greater miracles. To live—to fly—to invest—to play—to write—to remember—as I try to capture in this new set of essays. Don't stop me now!*

\* Tonight
I'm gonna have myself a real good time
I feel alive
And the world, I'll turn it inside out
Yeah!
I'm floating around
In ecstasy

So don't stop me now, don't stop me
'Cause I'm having a good time, having a good time

I'm a shooting star leaping through the sky
Like a tiger defying the laws of gravity
I'm a racing car passing by
Like Lady Godiva
I'm gonna go, go, go
There's no stopping me

I'm burning through the sky
Yeah!
Two hundred degrees
That's why they call me Mister Fahrenheit
I'm traveling at the speed of light
I wanna make a supersonic man out of you

Don't stop me now
I'm having such a good time
I'm having a ball
Don't stop me now . . . .

*Freddie Mercury*

# ASSAYING MONTANA

*I've been saving this little play on words for years: Montana Assays as Montana Essays. It seems so apt for us and for our history. So I'm tickled to finally use it!*

*The process and the metaphor of assaying, of course, come to us from ancient times. Old Testament Jeremiah describes God's sorting process: "I have made you an assayer and tester among my people that you may know and assay their way. They are bronze and iron, and they act corruptly." Jeremiah 6. But long before and after Jeremiah, humans were assaying—testing. Establishing the content of something precious from its surrounding dross. Testing ore to find gold and silver. Testing blood to sieve out antibodies or antigens.*

*Assaying is, in short, the several steps, the magical, often secretly guarded alchemy to render out base metals and find in their wake that which is prized. Through the millennia, assaying has been not just a science. It's a painstaking series of trial-and-error examinations. An art never fully learned—itself always being tested and retested.*

*White man's history of Montana settlement began with the rapacious search for gold. With the hope that our mountains and streams would cough up riches beyond anyone's wildest imaginings. We'd already trapped and hunted and fished the waters and forests and plains of this high plateau. And while that yielded beaver hats and adventurous tales, the next crop of men wanted more. And so they brought little beyond their greed and hope, pouring into our gullies and gulches. And assay offices followed them: Bannack, Virginia City, Elkhorn, Argenta, then Helena and Butte.*

*Had, of course, all those early miners learned that the ore they dug and blasted from our hills was worthless, they wouldn't have stayed. Or attracted the next generation of settlers to overpower and destroy our real treasure: the native peoples who'd lived here for millennia.*

*Essays are cousins of assays. Their Latin roots share the intent of trying and weighing and testing and measuring. But in words rather than fire and chemicals.*

*In Montana tradition then, with just the credentials of living here 40 years, being at home here, laboring to preserve something of our past, here are some of my efforts at assaying our value—Montana's idiosyncrasies, gifts, failings. In essays, of course.*

# End of the Line

In 1980, two months after I moved to Montana, I had to return, briefly and quickly, to Washington D.C. for a hearing. Except I couldn't. I got there and back, but not quickly. Or easily.

Through the previous decade, I'd traveled across the US multiple times for National Park Service presentations and meetings. I'd navigated rental cars in San Francisco and show-me tours along the East Coast. I could leave my office in D.C. and take a taxi to Washington National (now Reagan) and be in—say—Phoenix before the day was over.

But after that trip back to D.C. as a Montana newcomer, I began to feel—to intuit—an unsettling image of my new home. I saw myself up high—on a plateau, surrounded by mountains. And hours and hassle away from the rest of the world. I felt a touch of claustrophobia.

Turns out, I experienced that shiver of entrapment for good reason. Montana's at the end of the line. We're the equivalent of a small Kansas town on a quiet spur line. Served by trains that arrive and depart in the middle of the night cause they have more important places to be during daylight hours. The milk-run railroad that my parents and grandparents once knew. The train connection that required waking in the middle of the night to get my mom started on her mission of mercy to Indiana. Or retrieve the minister home from his church conference in Illinois.

Rather without realizing it, I'd moved to a high and dry, isolated and insulated land. Where geographic location and weather and topography forever determine our lives—my life. Nor was I helped by purchasing a cheesy condo that overlooked downtown Helena but still huddled in the shade of foothills above me.

Buffalo fed and clothed and sheltered Montana's original inhabitants. As if—in all their enormous shaggy splendor—the animals had been created for this place. Able to adapt. Forever moving. When Lewis and Clark traveled up the Missouri, they recorded wildlife at every turn and a few native people. But they didn't find a waterway to the

Pacific as President Jefferson had hoped. There was no gentle crossing of this vast interior land. Instead, they faced two more punishing mountain ranges.

The trappers and miners who followed in their wake found treasures—that they then couldn't sell easily to the rest of the world until the federal government began subsidizing transcontinental railroads. The Northern Pacific finally spanned Montana in 1883.

Our enormous acreage is glued to the Canadian border for 500 miles. In today's cars, we're a day's drive from Seattle, four from New York. Our average elevation is 3300 feet above sea level.

In 1980, fewer than a million folks lived within our expansive boundaries. We're now at a booming 1.1 million. A dozen US **cities** exceed or come close to our entire population.

So planes, trains, and buses make no money serving Montanans. There are too few of us and too few of us traveling. The distances from here to any "there" are immense. There are no economies of scale. And winter weather adds yet another impediment.

Bozeman is something of an exception. It now caters to the millionaires who fly in on the way to their second homes in the Paradise Valley or come for skiing in Big Sky. It boasts a play-pretend urban airport—parking prices and snarls to match. Missoula, Billings, and Glacier/Kalispell are getting busier for similar reasons.

But for sure, Helena's still the land of the last-in at night and first-out in the morning. If our connecting flight is at all delayed, we're doomed to watch Montana planes—the last leg of a journey—taxiing out from their ramps. The flights that make "on time" departures from Seattle and Salt Lake and Denver, too often leave us back at the courtesy desk bargaining for a room voucher. And while in 1980, I could travel from Helena to D.C. through Minneapolis, that route has disappeared.

Here, for the capital city, just three airlines arrive and depart. And only this year—after my 40 years of residence—can you actually board and deplane on all flights through a jetway. Prior to that, we braved snow and wind to climb into various small half-prop planes. We enjoy no airfare deals. No big-city to big-city bargains or flash sales.

End-of-the-line has also meant the death knell of sweet travel anonymity. Initially, I'd found it charming—in Helena's baby airport—that the governor secured his own luggage. Then it became unnerving to realize that someone I knew or recognized would inevitably be in the Salt Lake or Seattle crowd trying to reach Helena. For many years, those of us traveling to an isolated, end-of-line place in the West, shared a frumpy, windowless Salt Lake waiting room far from an airport bookstore or the Cinnabon stall. Plus the likelihood of having to chat with folks we sort of knew.

For some golden years before the interstate system began to creep across the nation, Montana was served by three transcontinental rail routes and a lacy network of spur lines. In the 1920s, one-room schoolteachers in the very center of Montana's range land could take a spur line train to Great Falls for a day to Christmas shop. And the three cross-country lines offered politicians and businessmen functional access to both coasts and especially Chicago and Minneapolis. Now, a remote schoolteacher must brave icy roads to do her shopping. And only a once-a-day, vastly unpredictable Amtrak passenger train traverses Montana—and does so across our least populated northern border.

We experience those "end of the line" realities in other ways. Amazon never managed two-day delivery for prime members. Here, count on seven. Forty-three states enjoy one or more Trader Joe's stores. We aren't one of them. The US Postal Service keeps quietly erasing post offices from small towns. And Helena mail—capital city that we are—does not leave from here, but from Great Falls 90 miles away. Now that our local paper is being delivered by mail, it takes a two-day joyride before delivery back here.

When I moved to Montana in 1980, I was 34 years old. This step was an adventure, an opportunity to learn a new place and a great variation on previous work. I assumed that I'd give Montana my all,

learn her gifts, and then sooner or later bite on another experience. I didn't count on Dave. And I didn't count on a place of such beauty, of history so perfectly reflected in landscape and buildings. Of a place without pretentiousness, ostentation. A place where those very end-of-the-line realities do not support flash and dazzle.

So, Montana has become my end-of-the-line. Like others of my age, I know that medical services here are OK but not great. If you live on ranches in central Montana, you've made peace with the absence of any speedy delivery to an emergency room. Senior living facilities are cookie-cutter corporate. While winter clothing and snow tires have all improved significantly in the 40 years, I know that short dark days and ice will determine where I go and what I do for more than half of each year. And, and I could no more afford to sell and buy elsewhere even if I wanted.

Still, the living out of the end-of-my days here in this high and remote country is no hardship. Soon, tonight, I'll water the geraniums and tomatoes on the porch and sit for a moment to look into our limitless sky.

**July 2023**

## Beyond the End of the Line: Compensating

Helena, Montana, is a very lovely, very small capital city. More a town in many ways. Our official population stands at 33,000, though surrounding suburbs now account for another 20,000 or so. We began life as a mining camp in the 1860s. Then after a transcontinental railway came to town, morphed into a finance and business center, a capital, a sedate and wealthy baby city. Victorian mansions and then small bungalows of multiple styles soon replaced false-fronted mining shacks. Over time, our diverse mining and rail population included African Americans, Native Americans, Chinese, and Jewish. We slowly became more homogenized. The State of Montana, Blue Cross/Blue Shield, and the hospital now employ the most Helenans. We're stubbornly middle class in income and taste.

Five other Montana cities are now larger and more sophisticated, at least in shopping and restaurants. And, as noted in the previous essay, some are a little less isolated by air transportation than we are. But not by much.

Helena, though, is truly at the end of the line. And to my way of thinking we've compensated, maybe even overcompensated for our little-sister, our relatively lonely, Plain Jane place in the world. We are a hotbed of culture. Of art, music, history, and literature. Of quirky creativity.

Take the Archie Bray Foundation. Which was once a brick and tile manufacturing business that the farsighted son of an owner saw as the perfect place for potters and sculptors to work. A world already built for transforming clay into art. The incredible buildings—some new, some historic, some falling into oblivion—have hosted an international set of students and instructors since the early 1950s. They have found their way—however awkward the route—to studios that inspire and a town that welcomes them. In fact, the Bray stays as firmly centered in Helena as it does the world. Bray students create flowerpots for Mother's Day "Pots and Plants" extravaganza. And bowls for an "Empty Bowls" nonprofit soup fundraiser. We wander among the new and old buildings at the Bray as well, alive with 70 years now, of cast-off pieces, seconds hidden among historic bricks and clay pipes, and alarmingly wonderful masterworks.

Our little Holter Museum of Art often teams up with the Bray. The museum/gallery is housed in a historic thick-walled stone warehouse built to store mining explosives. Early in Helena's history, the Holter family founded a freighting empire, transported ore overland and down the Missouri River to St. Louis and returned with mining, milling, and lumber supplies and hardware for a booming territory. Third generation Norman "Jeff" Holter participated in creating and testing atomic weapons in the 1950s and then, in a small Helena laboratory, developed the Holter Heart Monitor. His widow Joan, herself a chemist, sparked and funded the creation of the Art Museum in the family's name. Although there are years when the Holter hangs on to existence by a thread, it has survived—offering a wide array of changing shows, classes for kids and seniors, and lovely space for receptions and programs. A freighting fortune transformed into art.

Helena's independent movie theater, Second Story Cinema, began in the 1970s—literally in a business block's upper story. New York-born Arnie Malina—attracted to Montana's hideaways and mountains—remembers, "We bought the seats from an old theater in Fort Benton and found an old popcorn machine... made the projection booth in what used to be a closet for a secretarial school." Malina and his partners booked two independent films a week in the 88-seat, jerry-rigged space, along with live programming. And then, in an even more daring move, rustled up the funds to acquire Lewis and Clark County's 1880s jail and renovate it into an astonishingly contemporary 300-seat performance center—the Myrna Loy Center. Which thrives still with two film showings an evening and a host of local and national performers. Those performers, of course, command hefty fees, but the theater's managers have mastered the art of piggy-backing Helena shows with those in neighboring towns. And securing donated motel space. We fill the theater. All of us, thumbing our noses at our isolation. Myrna Loy, by the way, grew up in Helena and is buried in one of our cemeteries.

You will have seen the pattern already: our blessed propensity to situate cultural organizations in Helena's historic buildings. Once more consider our local, grassroots Grandstreet Theater. The building began in 1901 as a Unitarian Church, morphed into the community library after an earthquake decimated its early home. Then in the 1970s, a tiny local theater company received the funds to convert the church/library back into an auditorium. Grandstreet fills its seats throughout the year with locally produced shows and runs a children's theater school.

So that library, the Lewis and Clark library, had moved from pillar to post before local citizens funded a new building in an area razed by Helena's urban renewal—early home to our Chinese residents, a red-light district, and tiny miners' cabins. Pure luck has brought us powerful, invested library directors who are always a step ahead of great ways to serve the community. We are rich in programming, book clubs, children's services, technology assistance, community reads, and meeting space available for many organizations. Like the Myrna, the library and its board lure well-known authors to town. Our independent bookstore reaps the rewards. We lean into world-renown word masters.

Though a state institution, the Montana Historical Society museum, library, archives, photo archives, and galleries offer the best of Montana history and art. While currently waiting for the completion of a brand new space, the staff still arranges a wide array of programming and school resources. The Society helps Montanans and travelers from around the world understand that Charlie Russell's art defines this place before ANY transportation allowed European Americans to settle.

The Montana Jewish Project has just reclaimed the earliest synagogue built in the West as an educational center. Four-year Catholic Carroll College provides superb music and theatrical performances—along with guest lecturers and the unrefined gold of senior papers. Helena supports a symphony and a chorale—even as we fundraise to bring in musicians and a conductor from urban areas—trying hard to find vocalists and musicians only one airline hop away.

I cannot accurately compare Montana with other states. But I'm inclined to believe that what I know in Helena defines the rest of this place: a summer stock, sold-out theater in the most unlikely spot in far northeastern Montana. Museums in virtually every county, many of them administered by volunteers who have taken time to secure training. Significant art and history galleries in every major city. A wildly vigorous humanities program that sends speakers to the corners of the state in all weathers—the honorariums lean but the travel reimbursements generous. Equally vigorous statewide public radio and television programs.

And then there's literature and artistry. Montana steadily produces dazzling authors and photographers and artists. Beyond the end of all the planes, trains, and automobiles—beyond easy access—in this enormous, rugged landscape, we birth and nurture people with a bent for the right word and the right camera angle and the glint of sun on mountains. These artists flourish in part because they encourage and celebrate each other. They value the community they find in small university towns and abandoned gold camps. And every last one of them thrives in and takes inspiration from the empty beauty of our landscapes. Being at the end of the line seems to set their skills on fire.

I'm thinking tonight of the price of tickets for Broadway shows or the Metropolitan Opera. Or the cost of getting to Washington D.C. to visit the National Gallery of Art or the Library of Congress or the Smithsonian. Much less flying to Europe or India. It's not that we are homebodies by nature or that we'll turn down travel opportunities. It just isn't easy. Money alone doesn't mitigate flights caught in Denver snowstorms or missed connections in Seattle. Or 18-hour jet lag. So thank goodness for all the energetic, starry-eyed folks who've built and supported the magic of the bright lights and ball gowns, the brilliant imagery and the best writing—right here.

**August 2023**

## Bad Behavior Under the Big Sky

In the autumn of 2022, Montanans—who, I swear, didn't quite realize what they were doing—managed to cherry pick the worst of our citizens for almost every political position available. There are, of course, some notable and noble exceptions. But across the board, we (used very euphemistically) checked our ballot boxes for money-grubbing, out-of-state or out-of-touch land and tech developers; bullies; right-wing religious fanatics; intertwined, interpaternalistic family members; creationists; crude followers of whatever out-of-state guidance they received from Christian nationalists.

Yes, we weren't an exception to the patterns of red-state behavior. But we aren't one. We've been better. We know better. For more than 75 years, we chafed under a copper collar. And its tentacles that held newspapers and politics in a death grip. We'd only begun freeing ourselves from that when the copper industry kicked us to the curb and walked out. And for a while, Montana found its practical, even inspired soul. We elected giants to many positions (think Mike Mansfield and Pat Williams and Lee Metcalf). And for others, we elected ordinary, pragmatic folks more interested in helping the state than kowtowing to party or narrow, bigoted interests.

So, our history alone should tell us not to put our fate in the hands of out-of-state, power-hungry politicians.

But we just did.

And what makes that capitulation to the Freedom Caucus (which, of course, advocated for everything EXCEPT personal or municipal freedom) even more bizarre—curious—outrageous is the very place we call home.

You and I have the privilege to live in Big Sky Country. The Land of Shining Mountains. The Treasure State. Never mind our national or state parks, you and I get groceries and fill up our gas tanks every day against a backdrop of lavish beauty. At the drop of a free afternoon, we can find ourselves a sweet stream, a picnic spot, a road on which we'll meet no one for an hour. Our evening sunlight rivals that of Italy—and we live in its gold. We are the story and the country that's inspired brilliant writers and, most recently, TV producers.

So you'd think, or at least I think, that this very place—this Last Best Place—would summon our better angels. Would inspire us to think kindly and broadly and freely when it comes to how we care for each other and this land.

I don't understand how—in the face of this landscape and our history—we allowed ourselves to be hornswoggled by pinch-faced, pinch-hearted people. By people whose focus is so bitter, so self-centered, so petty that they ignore the true treasures of this place. Along with the ordinary people whose ancestors have lived here since time immemorial and newer families who came to try their luck—not really for a quick buck (though the miners hoped) but just for a safe, steady life.

I don't understand how people who claim to be extra-Christian, to be much holier than the rest of us, can justify their narrow mindedness. Their cruelty. Their self-righteousness. Against a backdrop of grand, ethereal mysteries and beauty that others pay lavishly to visit.

Some summer Sunday nights in my prairie hometown of McPherson, Kansas, our congregation met in Lakeside Park instead of the church. Our vespers honored the natural world. In that unremarkable Midwestern picnic spot replete with lonely ducks, quiet water breeding mosquitoes, a breeze in the cottonwoods, we began by singing:

*God, who touchest earth with beauty,*
*Make me lovely too;*
*With Thy Spirit re-create me,*
*Make my heart anew...*

*Like the arching of the heavens,*
*Lift my thoughts above;*
*Turn my dreams to noble action,*
*Ministries of love.* *

And we ended with:

*Day is dying in the west;*
*Heav'n is touching earth with rest;*
*Wait and worship while the night*
*Sets her evening lamps alight*
*Through all the sky.* \*

Sung reverently, acapella, four-part harmony.

I can no more imagine our current slate of Freedom Caucus folks being able to say or sing those words. Or feel the awe and gratitude laced through them. Or bring to their work the gentleness and "noble action" that this state's beauty prompts.

For me, those heartfelt sentiments—to stand in awe and to honor Montana and the people who've come to make a life here—become the litmus test for where my votes will land. I am not impressed by the pretenders who pray for show on street corners, who wield smugness rather than understanding, who boast mansions and personal jets but spend no time caring for the least among us, who ridicule and exclude and harm anyone whose beliefs and background they do not share.

Vicious charlatans. Villains posing as principled. Whose behavior desecrates this most remarkable place.

**July 2023**

\*Hymns: God Who Touchest Earth with Beauty, Composer C. Harold Lowden, Author Mary S. Edgar;  Day is Dying in the West, Composer William Fiske Sherwin, Author Mary A. Lathbury.

## Acceptance

This is an old song—for a new but disappearing summer.

The berries, on Mary's mountain ash, have begun their transubstantiation.

From green to gold to orange. The mystery, the sacrament will end in

scarlet. The blood of winter.

Other rituals, other communions are less distinct. Dark that rushes into evening earlier and earlier. The daily degree-by-degree tiptoe toward cool. Marigolds and zinnias at their most exuberant. Petunias struggling to birth their last blooms. Swimming pools closed. School sales replaced by Halloween frippery.

I am at once content and wistful. The kitties make themselves at home. Beloved friends are packing to visit as I write. Baby tomatoes ripen. Root beer floats still taste of paradise. Newly washed windows stand open. Magpie parents gossip. Their teenagers hopping awkwardly nearby. I hear the rhythmic staccato of nail guns on roofing projects. "NOW, NOW, NOW."

Have I really lived 75 sweet summers? Knowing the exquisite pleasure of a house swept fresh as dark comes. The elixir of ice water. The blessing of a faint breeze across the dishpan. The generous sweat of work. Sunsets shared. Thunder. Lightning. A river of hail across the porch.

So once more a priceless summer. Rich in laughter and little children and longtime friends and hugs. A Manhattan made to perfection. These exquisite kittens. Books whose steel-edged writing took me to the darkness and detail of World War II and whose soft curves to the light of rivers and oceans and otter.

Once more I risk squeezing the hours too tightly. Wanting so much that I'll lose the gentle grace of this season.

More than ever, then, I need the sacrament of acceptance. My own metamorphosis from summer heat to winter sleep. Sun-warmed to house-sheltered. I've tried the "little engine that could" philosophy—a hollow vow that I never really meant.

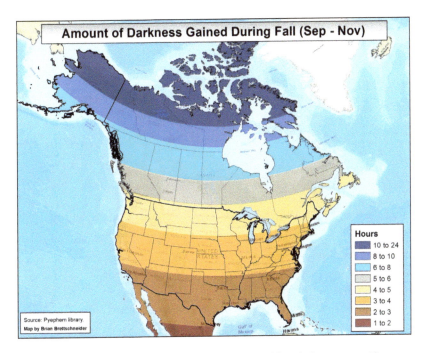

Amount of Darkness Gained During Fall (Sep - Nov)

Hours
- 10 to 24
- 8 to 10
- 6 to 8
- 5 to 6
- 4 to 5
- 3 to 4
- 2 to 3
- 1 to 2

Source: Pyephem library.
Map by Brian Brettschneider

I'll do better, I think, being honest with myself and the season. I'm not alone being drawn to our miraculous summers; our heart-stopping landscapes that tell so many stories. And this summer those riches came without smoke. I could go to bed with my mountain panorama standing guard.

I'm not alone, either, in my aversion to what's coming soon. Cold. Our season of cold is long. While you may still be raking leaves at Halloween, we've likely swaddled our children in long underwear and still require them to wear their coats and boots over costumes. And when you're cutting daffodils in March and April, I'll be shoveling snow and purchasing bouquets at Safeway. Dark. Not Alaska dark—but deep nonetheless. Dark that will eat up the morning and evening. Leaving us with a low, struggling sun during work hours. Ice. We are not the champion snowfall state either. But in our weather patterns, snow and miserly warmth intertwine to leave us icy footings. Among my friends, we know which businesses clear their parking lots and which let neglect create skating rinks.

And yet, I would not leave.

So once more, I will try for acceptance. For a celebration of what is. For a ceremony honoring understanding—as I've tried to learn my whole damn life—that I cannot have it all. That what I have is priceless. That through incredible good fortune and defiance I found myself in a magical place.

August 2022

## Safely Gathered In

This year, the universe has served up an uncommonly lovely fall. We have had flickers of frost some mornings. We struggled with a week of wildfire smoke. We got a bit of rain. Enough to make planting the snow stakes pretty easy.

But for almost a month now, we've enjoyed a deliriously lovely fall. The sky, framed by brilliant gold trees, remains breathtakingly blue. The geraniums on the porch bloom exuberantly. The coleus plants show no signs of withering. I caught a robin hopping merrily down our driveway just now—even more optimistic than I am. The Montana light has taken on Tuscany's gold clarity.

Winter's coming, of course. The city road crew has positioned orange plastic barrels of sand at corners known for icy accidents. Lawn and gardening companies are toting ancient air compressors—used just once a year—around Helena to blow out sprinkler systems. Rattletrap pickups have emerged from sheds—rusted, rebuilt in uncoordinated color panels from junkyard corpses. Ready—on a wing and a prayer—for hunting season or to be fitted with a plow blade for snow. Interstate 15's busy with Canadian RV's bound for Arizona sun. Automotive shops plead with us to come in now—before any flakes fly—to get our studded tires put on.

This month has also served up unremitting notices of mortality. Too many friends mourned the deaths and illnesses of people my age or younger. My calendar turned over to 76. The best-of-show birthday card I received reads: *"Age tends to silently swoop in like a bird of prey hunting you down and awaiting your squeal. Run!"* Whatever nonsensical confidence I had 30 years ago in believing that I would wake up the next day, now, if I'm honest with myself, the odds have changed. I move inexorably toward an end to my days. To no more tomorrows. To debilities that arrive unbidden in the dead of night and stay. To decisions about how and where to live that best be realistic. So how could each of these todays not be more precious. Why on earth would I want to spend them dreading—really anything.

More than being granted this uncommonly beautiful month or blindly ignoring my winter phobia, I have come around a corner from bare acceptance to gratitude. Independent of the weather, I think. To feeling more than ever that I am just hugely, exquisitely fortunate. To have today. To be alive. To be able to read. To write. To see—with (fingers crossed) macular degeneration generally at bay. To hear—especially after the audiologist tuned up my hearing aids today. To savor Tuxedo's and Tiger Tiger's affections and shenanigans. (I've taken to calling Tiger Tiger the Vampire. At night he bounds into bed to lick, knead, and nibble on my neck.) To know that my cranky knees do not keep me from savoring every winter day. More than anything, to slide into bed warm and safe. And to be able to help a very few other humans and animals know a bit of that sanctuary.

Catch me if I'm wallowing in winter grumpiness. Remind me of my great good fortune.

October 2022

## Hibernation

That's where the words have gone. Some special "extended state of torpor." Some deep drop in the metabolism of language and memory. Shocked into an energy-saving indolence. A lethargy designed to evade these dark days. To save up strength and stamina for a season that is not so spirit-robbing.

That's where my words have gone. Right along with organized ideas.

Right along with an animating ardor for beliefs that I want to share with the world. At the moment, these icy winds have stilled my mind, my reasoning, stolen the air out of my enthusiasms and blown them all to the badlands of the Missouri. Or maybe on to North Dakota oilfields. Some bleak landscape where—for now—they're hung up on a leafless cottonwood or an abandoned derrick.

So, tonight, the boys and I will tuck up in our cozy home. Tiger Tiger will find me wrapped in the silk of a woolly blanket and take up his favorite nuzzling spot on my chest. Favor me with Eskimo kitty kisses—serious nose rubbing. And love-scratched hickeys. While Tuxedo will meow for a spot of cuddling—throw himself down on the bed, stretch out on his back, invite sensuous tummy rubs. Or bring me the rattiest cloth mouse he can find for a game of fetch. Seriously. I am so lucky.

The words and memories, I suspect, will return—will wake—when I least expect them to. Maybe when I've finished sorting files or coming to grips with my closet. Winnowing through all those herbal remedies whose efficacies I've long since forgotten. Acknowledging the books I won't read again. Maybe then, winter's desolation will ease. Maybe the words in my brain will perk up and shake off the doldrums of this darkness.

And maybe a chinook blowing down off the Front will find all those lost ideas, the errant memories and send them back on a semi heading west. On a huge load of baled hay coming this way. And they'll return to Helena, to Alpine Drive.

**January 2023**

## The Sly Season

May first in Montana; May Day.

Spring, or so the calendar has said since late March.

But we know better here.

Now is not the time to hang the snow shovel in the garage

Or trade studded tires for summer ones

Or put the blankets in their cedar chest.

Much of the world may have burst into fulsome blooms, expansive lilacs and forsythia; ranks of tulips and red bud.

Here I'm just thankful for the midnight sprite who took yesterday's sprinkle and painted the drab grass a timid shade of green.

For the lonely bunch of daffodils at the foot of a neighbor's mail box.

For the brave and buoyant meadowlark at the edge of town, singing.

For the skittish buds on the mountain ash. Today? Too soon? Too late, they ask.

We have robins now, but they've been forewarned that the weather bureau still shows snow in the coming week;

Which—on our best days, when the sky is clear and the wind calm—will allow the Forest Service to fire up one more controlled burn and bathe the valley in smoke.

As the calendar also says, our days begin early and I treasure the glow of our indigo bedtime sky.

But this long light is bittersweet. It's the speeding march of our distant sun to its brightest, longest passage above us.

That will end just as our summer begins.

When we must accustom ourselves to the interminable journey of disappearing incandescence.

This is the sly season. The tricky season—at once both what we crave and what we crave too much. What we clutch tight-fisted lest it slides back into winter. Or lest it romps to its end before we've even enjoyed the idea.

And, in the polite conversation of check-out stands and neighborly calls, we speculate on summer—and whether there will be one. Or whether, once more, the mountains we love, the huge sky that shelters us will disappear again into the smoke of our troubled, tropical planet.

May 2022

## A Tribute Especially for Tony

Never underestimate the universe's brilliant, complex, and astonishing perversity.

Salish Elder Tony Incashola and long-ago friend and historian Bob Utley both died on June 7. Their deaths—and their lives—shadowed June. I knew each in different circumstances. Different geographies. Different times. Both devoted their lives to history and cultural and historic preservation. Both enjoyed the respect of many followers. And they were—in their passions and professions—diametrically opposite.

In an interview two years ago, Bob declared himself to be a Custer addict. In his 92 years, he published 23 books on the history of the American West. All but one circled around the color and conflicts of the 19th century. And much about the U.S. government and the U.S. Army as they did their level best to eradicate the native inhabitants of the American West or at least corral them into unforgiving patches of land. Although some of Bob's prodigious output focused on Native leaders and their heroic, ill-fated fight for survival (Sitting Bull and Geronimo in particular), Bob's life's work began and ended in the same place: a near adoration of the men in blue uniforms.

~ ~ ~

Tony was born on the Flathead Reservation in western Montana. Raised by his grandparents in material poverty but the cultural richness of traditional Selis-Qlispe circumstances. His mother died when he was a little over a year old. Tony—Antoine—grew up immersed in his traditional native language.

In 1966, a 20-year-old Tony came back from his Army deployment in Vietnam to bring his brother's body home. By 1974, Tony was married and beginning to raise a family. And, at the behest of a Salish elder who had the foresight to realize how endangered the Salish language and lifeways were, Tony began his life's work to preserve the language and culture of his people.

Initially, he struck out on his own to visit land areas sacred to the tribe (much of which had been taken from them by the U.S. government); identify traditional foods and medicines; follow early trails; conduct interviews with elders; begin recording voices and vocabularies that were on the edge of extinction. All the while, with an archivist's instincts, taking careful notes.

In the later 1970s, as governmental entities began their required consideration of cultural places and values, Tony's work and foresight morphed into a Salish Culture Committee. He directed the Committee most of the rest of his life. The Committee and its staff continued to document historic places, record the Salish language and Salish language speakers, unearth and catalog historic photos, find ways to engage Salish young people in the preservation of their culture.

And as Montana worked to implement its constitutional requirement to introduce all students to Native history and culture, Tony and the Committee became educators. Helping others select information, stories, and images that would introduce Montanans to Salish lifeways.

Every single Culture Committee responsibility put Tony in the position of being an advocate, a spokesperson, a mediator, a messenger, a counselor for his people. Often for the whole tribe. Often in the midst of racial and political and land management tension.

Tony was one of the first indigenous leaders I learned to know when I came to Montana in 1980. Over the years, our Preservation Office worked with every Montana tribal culture committee and many native educators. There was frequently an edge in our dealings. Standard archaeological practices often threatened traditional values. Landscapes were as important to indigenous people as our cathedrals—a concept hard to wrangle within regular historic preservation protocols. We stumbled over each other's vocabularies and strategies for handling meetings and meeting preservation law.

Through all of that, in ways that set an example for all other tribal contacts, Tony remained calm, not angry; gentle, not indignant. Willing to go the extra mile in explanations. Able to grasp ways to integrate tribal beliefs and practices with those of federal and state preservation regulations.

Tony was invariably soft-spoken, articulate, able to perceive the framework of a meeting or an audience and meet people where they were. He remembered individuals he had worked with—and their particular personal and professional situations. His passion caught fire with other Salish educators and preservationists. Unassuming, patient, humble, courteous, Tony led always by example.

All of this while Tony raised an expanding family—welcoming children from a variety of circumstances. While he found time and energy to follow local and state football and basketball teams. While he took time to be in touch with people who needed a word of encouragement. I was the recipient of one such note and call.

During Covid, Tony adopted Zoom and other electronic ways of carrying out his work. Right up until the end. "He loved his work," Peone-Stops [a Culture Committee colleague] said. "He didn't think of it as a job; he saw it as his responsibility. And he was happy to do it to ensure our people know who they are and know where they come from." And from his hospital bed: "When culture committee staff visited in the hospital the day before he died, he shared with them one last piece of advice, 'Continue.'"[+]

～ ～ ～

The coincidence, the fluke of Bob and Tony's deaths—on an early June day as our world doubles over in paroxysms of war and famine and flood and fire and tyranny—caught my heart. Startled me. I can wrench only some wisdom from that twist of fate—if that's what it was. For sure, the fluke provided me with the opportunity to understand the gift of friendship I'd been given by two disparate humans. Maybe, maybe most of all, to realize the special good fortune of finding myself in Montana and being given the opportunity to learn about and from this landscape's original inhabitants.

July 2022

[+]*Nora Mabie, Indigenous Community Reporter, Lee Newspapers*

## Night Lights

After the first times I needed to pee at three in the morning at the Walter family's primitive North Fork of the Flathead property, I learned what the rest of the family already knew. I didn't go around behind the cabins to the outhouse unless I absolutely had to. There being no guarantee that wildlife of various sizes and temperaments wouldn't join me. Instead, I hustled out the cabin door, tried to remember other folks' preferred tinkle spots, moved a yard or two away, and squatted.

And then looked up.

To a night sky of such clarity and light and drama that I found it hard to breathe. I'd never seen—never ever seen—the universe, the infinity as three-dimensional, the stars as iridescent, the Milky Way as unmistakable. With a frisson of motion and sound and presence there in the pure dark stillness of The Land. The Earth moving.

No planetarium has ever come close. No other place I've been rivaled that night view.

The International Dark Skies Initiative has long since been educating and admonishing us to realize the treasure of night skies undimmed by human light. In fact, it tracks the earth's darkest places. Its succession of night-time aerial views of North America reveal the few remaining landscapes in our country where sodium vapor pinks, fluorescent blues, halogen headlights, and LED bulbs don't outshine the heavens. Montana once was one of those great, black spots on the map. The land east of the Mississippi River and along the Pacific Coast showed almost continuous nighttime light. The Louisiana Purchase registered darkest—punctuated by Denver and Salt Lake City. That reality is changing.

For many years, our million Montana folks could all see the night sky. Could glory in the prickly clean light of stars, the sweep of the Milky Way, the shimmery silk of Northern Lights. We trusted each other enough to turn out all our lights at night. REA, the Rural Electrification Association, was slow to reach some of us. When they did, our wattage wasn't all that high. We found cold dark winter evenings and light-rimmed summer nights peaceful, soothing, friendly. We could drive early interstates and two-laners through quiet hours and little traffic. Occasionally seeing the small humming glow of a tiny town or the cloud-reflected lamps of a Montana "city." From the air, we could name our tiny settlements and dying homestead clusters. No long, fat necklaces of high beams and fast food parking lots. No metropolises that stretched to the horizons.

In some places in Montana that's still true. Along the Hi-Line, for instance. Inside Glacier-Waterton. But not everywhere. Now our landscape of ranchettes bristles with yard lights. Our cities ooze out into their adjacent valleys and drape over prized hillsides. A land once silhouetted in moonlight is all too often dulled with domestic security poles and subdivision streetlamps. Commercial corridors defined in harsh fuchsia and neighborhoods in blue and white greet us as we top a highway hill leading into town.

Montana is not alone in this steady accretion of night lights. But we ought to be among the slowest, the most cautious. Given our sparse population, we enjoyed the night's best show longer than most. We are among the places on this earth where many of us remember what we are now losing.

What are we afraid of? What goes on in the dead of Montana nights now that our parents and grandparents did not fear or feel the need to illuminate? Is crime escalating? Have roving gangs of villains left us that much more vulnerable?

Is it the pressure we feel when the salesman tells us that our neighbor just got lights for the whole barnyard? When "as seen on TV ads" tout the security of LED motion activated garage lights? Where our planned condo associations or subdivision boards just like the look of lighted porches? What if we flipped the porch light on for our returning kids closer to their arrival time? What if we said no to the false security arguments of a condo board? What if we asked box stores to darken their parking lots? What if we made those conscious decisions?

The perils of turning nights into daylight are many. Plants and animals require earth's daily cycle of light and dark rhythm to live. They eat and sleep and hunt and hide and reproduce in a rhythm dictated by the earth's rotation away from and into light. Migrating birds, disordered by artificial glow, fly off course and crash into buildings. Millions of insects commit suicide in our ever-brighter lights, dying before they've accomplished their pollinating duties. We waste energy at a time where its production fuels global warming. Ask anyone with cataracts how deadly brilliant lights are. Even our belief that we outwit crime is false and renders us complacent.

In Montana, we are all, Native and European Americans alike, close to the millennia when fires and candles and oil lamps lighted our days. And when the moon and stars lit our nights. When the incredible nighttime expanse of universe and the mysteries that we've only begun to unravel brought us awe. When the stark contours of neighboring mountains set against a star-lit sky comforted us—assured us we were home.

My arthritic knees render squatting to pee in the wee hours of the morning a thing of the past. But standing out in pure North Fork dark still stays my heart. I join an enormous and endless riddle. Light from all the suns in the sky has given me life—and finally will return me to pure energy. Along with every other sentient being on the earth.

We treasure our big sky. And all too often think of it in its jaw-dropping daytime vastness—billowing clouds giving depth to a blue eternity that stretches beyond our eyes. Time, perhaps, to worship our cobalt midnight skies and their star-bright night lights.

**August 2021**

# Empty – Full

My British friends Jean and Bryan arrived in Montana on the remnant Amtrak passenger train, the Empire Builder, on a summer Saturday evening. The 48-hour trek west had been strange enough. Traveling in regular coach, the Sheldons hadn't realized that once they relinquished their luggage in Chicago, they wouldn't see it again until Shelby. Half of the country traversed and not even a toothbrush. So they were weary, hungry, and little more hygienically challenged than they'd hoped.

Beyond excited that they'd arrived, I assured them that our night's luxurious B & B, the Stone School Inn, lay just around the corner. Valier, as you may know, is about 30 miles south and west of Shelby on a combination of interstate and two-lane roads. An easy drive especially with the Front Range of the Rockies as backdrop.

About 20 minutes in, I could hear Bryan mutter "around the corner!"

Gather up the disparate islands of the United Kingdom and lay them gently inside Montana's capacious borders. Not only will England and Northern Ireland, the Isle of Skye, Wales, the Highlands of Scotland fit into Montana. More than a third of our state will be left over—perhaps all the western valleys—ancient Lake Missoula riding the crests of ridge lines beyond the Rockies toward the Pacific. To Montana's 147,000 square miles, Britain comprises just 94,000.

And after you've settled the UK inside Montana, consider people. There are barely a million Montanans staking a claim to this particular state. There are 67 million inhabitants of the British Isles.

We—European Americans—arrived on this continent from tiny, densely populated countries beyond the Atlantic 400 or more years ago. We poured first onto the continent's eastern shores and then pushed further and further inland. We were propelled from Europe by famine and industrialization and persecution. We were lured away by the hopes of better living, of being needed, of freedom to work and worship as we chose. We lived the same push and pull within our own continent—from East to West. We managed to create a country brewed from ideas, philosophies, dreams, cravings.

By an incredible combination of hubris and circumstance, European Americans laid brutal claim to these lands and have had the illusion of believing that we breathe freer here than we might anywhere else. And that we are somehow entitled, that the universe or a god granted

us the right to an unending supply of the riches that came with the land. We made that assumption and acted on it at the price of millions of Native lives and the unbearably brutal treatment of millions more.

Here, in this upper Rockies, high plains land, for sure, I enjoy the gifts of light and space and colorful dimension. I love our relative quiet. Often, during Jean and Bryan's visit, we traveled two-lane highways for an hour and never saw cars or people. The Sheldons rafted the North Fork of the Flathead River and passed incoming streams where the trout and white fish had never heard human voices. We spotted momma cow and calf pairs laying claim to their very own ten acres of grazing land. We attended concerts lit by extraordinary sunsets and full moons, in diamond clear air.

We traveled to Glacier and Yellowstone. To my eyes, beautiful island kingdoms crawling with tourists. To the Sheldons, exotic beauty. The Last Chance Stampede Rodeo with all its pageantry and dust and danger dazzled. Even as an orchestrated, overwrought commercial version of the work cowhands accomplished on an open range. We attended the Montana Kootenai Tribe's pow wow, perhaps Bryan and Jean's favorite experience. A ceremony beloved by tribal members. And still a stark study of a people's hard won struggle to preserve and celebrate some of their many lost traditions.

Truth: Jean and Bryan fell in love with Montana. Exuberantly, thoughtfully, permanently. And yet, along with our sky and land which tell their own stories, I had served up for them vignettes fashioned from the myths we love to live, but myths nonetheless.

Our world on this side of the pond and on this side of the Mississippi runs on squares—on land that the government parceled out predictably and precisely. Starting with latitudes and longitudes, surveyors brought their alidades and engineers' chains to the endless, unbroken spaces between the old Midwest and all of the Louisiana Purchase. And ruled it off as if we were a sheet of graph paper. To ferry Jean and Bryan to Valier, we drove due south and then turned due west following those surveyed lines. We sped by land given away by the federal government—so sure were we of the endlessness of it. Almost from the beginning, homestead legislation afforded settlers ownership just for the price of toughing it out and cultivating land. In fact out here, the feds were slow to realize that homesteaders could survive only on bigger and bigger plots.

Visitors pay outfitters to wrangle them up into three and half million acres of wilderness. Our towns sprawl to the limits of topography or of employment. We fashion house after house out of wood—on sizeable urban lawns or several acres of land. We add subdivisions and spawn ghost towns all at the same time. The Forest Service torches slash piles late fall and early spring. We watch hundreds of square miles burn every summer—or beetles turn range after range into a sickly red. In our search for precious metals, we poison aquifers with arsenic and believe—not correctly—that the land and our children will forgive us a little longer.

We were sold—or given—a bill of goods; blinded by our own fantasies; too sated and self-serving to realize that the abundances had limits and cost dearly.

Three years after Jean and Bryan's visit here, I joined them in their home and their West Sussex landscape—a bit of England between London and Brighton in the southeastern corner of the country. Half a million years ago, hominids lived there. Neolithic humans mined flint from the Sussex Downs. Then, in succession, a Roman canton, Celtic country, a Saxon kingdom, a Norman stronghold, a medieval territory of castles and cathedrals and conquests from within and without. Now, Sussex is a county, informally divided into West and East. The greenery-swathed, winding lanes that we traversed between villages were created by deer and cattle and then pilgrims and soldiers and royals. Native stone

buildings that spanned those centuries remain cheerfully occupied.

Marked by successive waves of human living and ruling and warfare, Sussex has been extraordinarily pivotal to British survival and history, however exposed to the world along its English Channel flank. There are 1200 Sussex residents per square mile to Montana's seven. That Sussex density, the length and breadth of that history, its survival across time and assault deliver cultural richness, stories and legends, artistry, layer upon layer of "this is the place" moments beyond anything I could comprehend.

To my eyes, its antiquity and population have spawned a conscience and carefulness of living and planning unknown here. Though Britain has its share of motorways, excessive highway rights-of-way consume little countryside. Roundabouts stitch lanes and roads and motorways together, rather than the enormous concrete cloverleaves of our interstates. Our lavish cut-and-fill curves rival those of the Indianapolis 500. And we think it our due to drive accordingly. Not in Sussex— where lightning-fast reflexes, reasonable speeds, courtesy, and confidence are required.

Though nothing like the amazing net of steam trains that once pasted the country together, trains and good bus services still keep Brits commuting and vacationing. Which is why, perhaps, Jean and Bryan expected more of Amtrak, Montana's only transcontinental passenger rail service, than it could deliver.

And in the UK, armies of volunteers, older men and women, have restored and operate steam trains and original depots across the country. Tourist dollars and holiday fun wreathed in clouds of steam and soot. In fact, volunteerism flourishes. Bryan's a Shedder. Named to recognize male Brits' historic attachment to humble backyard buildings perfect for having a smoke and a moment alone, Bryan's Shed buddies do repairs and odd jobs for locals who need assistance.

To prune or remove a tree in Sussex, you ask permission from the County Council. "Wooden" houses are rare; brick and local stone more common. Manufactured lodges cluster in planned and zoned holiday parks. Villages defined by "high streets" are lined with historic buildings and grow carefully. Folks still live above their shops. Ranchettes have not crowded out real farms. Small gardens survive in front or back of many homes, planted to vegetables in World War II. "Council" houses are still being built to meet residential needs. Extensive biking, bridle, and hiking paths cross private land, coexistence made manageable by rules for both users and owners. Birds and animals are often protected or safeguarded from inhumane hunting or capture. Even fox hunting has had its proverbial wings clipped. Historic preservation's driven not just in adherence to rules and sentimental emotions, but because it's economical and functional. Every square inch of land and many social systems reflect consciousness and courtesy so that at once, many people, their history, and natural resources can survive into an indefinite future.

Remember, I was in Sussex on this visit for two weeks. With my own biases and expectations. Big box stores and graceless housing developments have emerged. Generalizations do no country justice. Still, to our carelessness, I saw caution. To our hubris, I saw matter-of-fact modesty of spirit and living. To our certainty that freedom means doing any damn thing we please, I saw recognition that cooperating makes for saner and better living for everyone. To our often expansive and expensive recreation (think off-road-vehicles, giant boats, behemoth motor homes), I saw plain and simple play and joy. A walk on the beach, a cup of coffee, a market. With the sheer density of people, the span of history, the need to navigate through millennia of tyrants—religious and political—I saw conservation, cleverness, artistry, cooperation.

Many Montanans cannot currently find an affordable place to live. Mobile homes, even recent models, are no match for our weather. Ranks of dismal apartment buildings appear in dismal places. Which begs the question: who among us actually needs 3,000 square feet to live and two sinks in one bathroom? Who of us cooks on six gas burners and three commercial ovens at one time? When did every member of a household require his or her own bathroom? When did our egos demand that we kill any species we can and display our butchered animals as trophies? When did we decide that we could slaughter any of God's creatures as cruelly as possible for sport or gluttony?

However hardscrabble our first white settlers were, however utterly dependent on the knowledge of the original inhabitants that we hounded into bare survival, however much our concerted effort to throw off the copper collar and reach a point of sensible independence, now... now Montana's joined the rest of the country in valuing glittery shows of wealth and hollow power over living our consciences.

How might we meet our incredible opportunities here? Our ill-gotten gains, but now ours nonetheless? Eternal gratitude perhaps? Awe that we have this gift of breadth and possibility? Less hubris and more humility and honesty? Living small under our big sky rather than rapaciously? Reckoning with the price for "taking" these lands from their original inhabitants? Joy. Determination to preserve the very qualities of natural resources and history and beauty to which we pay homage.

No place and no people are perfect. I am home here now. I glory in Montana's history and broad landscape. I am a big sky, big country, small town girl. I try hard to spend reflecting time on my porch, at a window with my long and lovely view to the Big Belts. And I am extraordinarily thankful for the opportunity to see how other countries, other people live their lives and their resolves and behaviors in ways that might also serve us. What might our huge empty state learn from a small, full country with an outsized history?

July 2021

## Views: From Here To...

This afternoon, I'm looking out to the east, watching the Big Belts. The 75-mile-long Rocky Mountain island chain stretches in an arc—a belt. Not quite 10,000 feet at its highest point. The Missouri River splits its canyon walls—the Gates of the Mountains, the Lewis and Clark Expedition called it. A modest range that figured centrally in the 1860s as miners rushed to its gulches for gold. Now we know it for timber sales, fires, grazing land, hidden log cabins, and the lovely, treacherous Deep Creek Canyon highway, the only paved road that spans the range.

The Big Belts, 20 or 30 miles away as the crow flies, frame my days—my mood, the day's evolution. Today, it's snowing sporadically along the range, a system steadily moving south. In the last hour, I watched the storm blossom and turn serious. So far here in Helena it's only windy. In the summer, curtains of rain inch across the mountains. At night, from my bed, I watch electrical shows and count the heartbeats before thunder scares the cats. On temperate days, the Belts send cumulus marshmallows up into the sky.

I am so enamored with the Big Belts and their drama that I am undone when our valley fills with smoke and inversions. Or when heavy snow blocks my view. It's not a perfect high mountain pristine perspective. It's not The Land. Here I look over apartment buildings and a scatter of houses near East Helena, a dot of red the local hockey rink. At night, the flash of police cars and ambulances. But I'm up high enough that the foreground falls away. I am left with sky and mountains.

~ ~ ~

At 830 North Ash in McPherson, Kansas—the home my folks bought in 1953—the view north dominated our lives. Lincoln Grade School and its bursts of playground activity. Then, two blocks beyond the ugly Farmers' Alliance insurance building, on up to the "new" water tower.

Its mushroom dome illuminated in white light most of the year and then, in December, changing Christmas colors. Three times a day, standing at the sink and kitchen window, we looked to the tower as we did dishes. In winter, in the dark, feeling comforted by a lighted landmark. And in an emotional dark, as my parents grew ill and less able, my sister and I gathered in the kitchen to talk over what to do next—the water tower a kind of Great Plains lighthouse that kept us steady through difficult choices.

My college dorm rooms had big windows sighted across our little campus—or to the neighboring church. But I was too busy at my desk or rendezvousing with friends to notice. During my guinea pig/ fever study summer, Bethesda and parts of Washington D.C. spread out below our sixth floor room. Absorbing that view was just part of the summer's fairy tale—too exotic to be believed.

I have no memory of charming views from my University of Oregon apartments. Just rain. And the insides of a metal study carrel in the library complete with cold, wet feet. The backside of another apartment building once I got home. And more rain.

In Gettysburg summers, Mrs. Keefer's blisteringly hot sunporch sat right on the sidewalk and I kept the shades pulled to block heat and tourist curiosity. The funky apartment I rented my teaching year—a series of bedrooms Roger and Olive had pasted into a shotgun unit when their daughters married—offered up bucolic Maryland countryside.

When I moved to Gettysburg for a permanent position, I stumbled into a magic home: a second-floor gable-roofed apartment next to the National Cemetery. An aerie settled in the tops of pine trees. No long views but sun and greenery. And the pure joy of having my own grown-up apartment. I owned a stereo, a bistro table, a bed, a Victorian love seat, and a few books and records. Perfect for a world in which the landscape that fueled my days was the battlefield itself.

Three years later I moved to work for the National Park Service in Washington D.C. I arrived for the changing of White House residents: Nixon out and Ford in. For the next six years, I lived in three different World War II era apartments—the last of which became a condo that I bought. Those interiors were lovely—parquet floors, butcher block counters, generous rooms. With gentle, green, comfortable shared "yards." But then and now, the landscapes that I loved are the monumental ones that I got to walk every day: across the Mall to Interior, uptown past the K Street offices, Judiciary Square that came into view as I rode the subway and escalator to the Pension Building.

I flew to Helena when I moved here. And by the time the big Mayflower truck arrived, I'd rented a flimsy condo in one of Helena's early neighborhoods. I looked to the west—up a scraggly hill or down the block to badly remodeled nineteenth century houses. Mostly, I lived physically and emotionally in the basement of the Montana Historical Society. Wrangling a hell of a new job.

Six years later, the spring Dave and I married, we toured Helena with realtor Bill Spilker to find the perfect bungalow for a family that now included Dave's daughters, Emily and Amanda. We found no such thing in our price range, but stumbled into a better option. A builder-constructed 1950 rancher—long on storage, small architectural graces, and the partially finished basement that Dave loved.

The front picture window faced south and framed Mount Helena—a saddle-topped half hill, part of a ridge of baby mountains. An interesting landscape, but not the one I remember most. As in McPherson, our midsize square of kitchen window became the portal to my world. It faced the backyard that had much influenced our purchase. An upper level with a huge lilac bush and garage; a lower level with patio/basketball free throw circle, raspberry bushes, garden, and the most elegant, enormous climbable Russian olive. Flower beds all around—scattered tulips, bleeding hearts, lilies of the valley, and tall delphiniums. A strawberry patch that became the rabbit cemetery. We fed the birds deliberately and the deer inadvertently. I spent summer evenings weeding—an enterprise good for my soul but never finished.

But I knew that backyard view best from the kitchen window. Cooking, doing dishes, packing school lunches, washing vegetables. Daydreaming, listening for the distant band concert, or watching for the faint sky-high scribbles of rodeo fireworks. Somehow I had a powerful, grownup marriage, a family home, the sweet routines of a homemaker, and the needing-to-take-a deep breath annoyances of any marriage. That Russian olive my steady anchor and friend.

~ ~ ~

Not quite two years after Dave died, I found this condo, fell in love with its layout and light and deep front porch. I was still working part-time, so settling in, understanding the neighborhood, getting art up on the walls happened slowly. I'm part of a three-building, 12-unit complex. Even then I knew that I'd struck gold. In my 2008 Winter Letter: *"I watch sun and moon-rise over the Big Belts; evening light shimmering on a silver band of Missouri River; and goofy gangs of yearling deer chasing each other along a ravine."*

In a world where so many of our fellow beings live on the street, in tents, in camps stretching across the desert, in basements already shell-shattered by war, I have been pure lucky—pure undeserving—of safe, suitable, interesting homes. Of the ability to savor exquisite places on our earth. In no part of my life have I lived in ugliness or fear. If I'd never moved here, I still would have enjoyed a lifetime of wonderful homes—and views. Every place seemed to fit its stage of my life.

As developers crank out low-income apartments in Helena, they build on unwelcoming but available plots and install as few windows as possible. Economies trump loveliness. Instead, what could be better for struggling families than light, airy creative design—greenery and sky and breadth. Never mind the realities of senior housing. Picture two-occupancy nursing home rooms and the dark, stuffy, claustrophobic bed on the inside wall. The single window beyond a curtain and closed anyway.

I grow more grateful and enchanted as I age. I have time now to look up from my books and cats and computer and take a deep breath, to register the beauty, the breadth and depth of the world. To track seasons by how far the sun rises above the peaks—and so how bright my home becomes. To acknowledge and salute the whole iridescent universe. To watch for reflected sunsets that dance along in gold and pink on eastern clouds or paint my Big Belts in mauve and purple. To follow a slender finger of light as it brings a gulch into sharp relief. To breathe.

If I am even more lucky, I will slide from this dazzling slice of our solar system to the stars beyond. From here to eternity.

**April 2023**

# HARVESTING MEMORIES

*Notwithstanding the scientists who've conducted memory experiments, the psychologists who've studied the meaning of memories, the thousands of memoirs printed, we still don't understand the phenomena of remembering. We know that memories are elusive. That no two siblings share the same ones. That deeply buried ones can suddenly emerge. And long held ones vanish. That they can be false—manufactured for a need. Always colored with the crayons of our circumstances.*

*But the sticky, tricky damnable reality of memory is that it defines us. Absent memories of ourselves and our place in the world, we are unmoored. We cannot function. We are, on the one hand, small warm-blooded machines. But the WE—the US—the I is a rich aggregation of memories that tells us who we have been, what we've done, and what we want and need and treasure and fear. Memories guide us, give us life. Stripped of them, we are dead in the water of our lives--paralyzed. Unable even to remember who and what we love.*

*In fact, as we live, we grow crop after crop of memories. Every day, every year we add to the storehouse of experiences and friendships and traumas and joys that comprise who we are. Truck loads, silos full, barns bursting with all that we've done and lived and thought.*

*So in these retirement years, I've got the time to consider the yields of my life. To relish the memories carried in my soul. To harvest the richest and quirkiest and enticing. To savor them. To feed off them. To use the flash of a sunflower or a line in a book to dig out odd recollections. To be struck by a news story or a turn of circumstances for which I need context. Or, however briefly, to live again inside toothsome moments. To sit with friends and colleagues whose deaths have left me bereft. To catch my breath as I walk inside the grandest building I've ever known.*

*What follows is a wide-ranging menu of memories—silly and sweetly serious.*

## Finding My...

High school debate reordered my life. Upended the way I looked at the world. Challenged my perceptions. But what was it that I found or discarded? What was the epiphany? Mostly I haven't spent the energy to parse the question—to understand the gift of that experience. I'll try.

First the basics.

For reasons I can't summon now, I signed up for debate my McPherson High School junior year. I can't have known much of what to expect. I was a predictable, straight-A, straight-laced, brown-nosing student. The only relevant experience I brought to the team came from 4-H competitive cooking demonstrations. Complete with cloth-covered card table, dainty apron, and an easel holding handmade signs. I made my mark in those demonstrations as the mistress of fancy biscuit making: basic dough—an orange-juice soaked sugar cube punched down in the middle. Voila, sweet orange biscuits. Butter and cinnamon sugar rolled into the mix—almost a cinnamon roll. Shredded Velveeta stirred in—cheesy biscuits. In hindsight, every kind of cheesy.

We were a tiny squad. A motley bunch with wide-ranging interests. Certainly different temperaments and differing locations on the school's popularity scale. Ordinary high school social life would never have brought us together.

The district had just hired Merle Ulery as the speech, drama, and debate teacher. A kind, dapper Southeastern Kansas man. Dazzlingly well-read. Comfortable in his own skin and story with a sharp eye for irony and humor. He respected high school kids and expected hard work and investment from us. We responded in kind. I would have sworn that he came from New York—so sophisticated and worldly he seemed—compared with our homegrown teachers.

The national high school debate topic that year seems to have been one of these three topics. For the life of me I can't remember which one we actually used. RESOLVED: *That the United States should promote a Common Market for the western hemisphere.* Or RESOLVED: *That*

TOP: Mr. Ulery, Dean Peer, Carl Frantz, Doug Mc-
Kenna, Kenneth Wilmoth, Benny Watson. BOTTOM:
Lynn Hafermehl, Carol Kaufman, Marcella Sherfy,
Anita Morlan, Charles Eklund.

the foreign aid program of the United States should be limited to non-military assistance. Or RESOLVED: That the non-communist nations of the world should establish an economic community. You get the idea. Something that sounded important, was vaguely plausible, and related enough to current issues that the topic could be researched in available material.

By the time we attended our first meet, we'd spent hours in the library with *Time Magazine, U.S. News and World Report, Vital Speeches*—really any current policy journal we could find; materials provided by the National Speech and Debate Association; old history books and international politics texts. With all that research, we each assembled a list of primary arguments for and against the resolution. We created divided notecard file boxes, stuffed on one side with footnoted quotations and presentation themes **for** the resolution and stuffed on the other, **against** the resolution. We had a similarly organized accordion file full of articles or longer quotations. Everything pasted in or hand-written or typed on a manual typewriter. Today, students walk into debate matches with laptops. We struggled in with armloads of paper.

Debate competitions in Kansas were day and a half affairs—arranged in tournaments at schools that could accommodate many participants. Five or six elimination rounds preceded Saturday afternoon final rounds. Competitors were required to present either affirmative or negative positions on a moment's notice. We didn't know which we would be assigned until we walked into each room.

Mr. Ulery taught us the magic of a large sheet of paper, readied for each match—divided into two big columns and several smaller columns—used to track the flow of the debate. We began by recording the main affirmative and negative arguments, each sides' rebuttals, and then issues we wanted to remember in the future. The format allowed us to SEE the way the arguments were unfolding—and be more certain of responding to positions that our opponents offered.

Mr. Ulery partnered me with Anita—a wry, beautiful, thoughtful, and more popular girl. Our differences became advantages. Mr. Ulery would walk us to matches, glance at the judges, and then decide which of us should sit on the outside edge of our table up on the stage: Anita with her shorter suit skirt if the judges included a young man or me with my longer wool jumper if the judges looked to be staid old English teachers. Valuable lesson there—just in and of itself!

Our whole team did well, but Anita and I wowed. We won most of our tournament rounds and were state novice champions. We each now have a trophy awarded that year, although the squad mascot—a big plastic Bullwinkle soap bubble dispenser—has vanished.

I would debate my senior year as well, but without the electricity and encouragement of Mr. Ulery who had left for another position. We tried NOT to answer, instead, to a morose, greasy-haired man, with whom we didn't even want to share the school car.

So how and why was I a different person on the far side of that first year? I enjoyed the camaraderie of classmates on overnight trips and in huddled strategy sessions. We came to know each other well. Regardless of gender, we could joke and commiserate without the typical boy/girl high school tension. I learned to think on my feet and to order words well and grammatically. I could track the flaws in another team's presentation. We were taught poise—to stand up straight at podiums and look the judges in the eye. Anita and I enjoyed success—measured by others' yardsticks. Mr. Ulery encouraged us to celebrate our victories and that stoked our creativity, our investment in the effort, and our egos. Ordinary routines and responsibilities took second place in our attentions.

But the sum of my change seems much larger and more essential than speaking skill or social ease. I came from a home and a growing up where modesty and self-effacement too often morphed into insecurity. Where humility became self-doubt. But from that debate year, I walked away with... agency. With a strength and confidence that's hung around in the years since. With confidence in myself that others' opinions can't vanquish. An "I can." And "I will." That strength and trust falters occasionally—sometimes a lot. The first semester of graduate school comes to mind. And some fearful spells here in this eighth decade when my body's unreliable. But I seem to return mostly to optimism and fortitude, even as I trim the sails of my activities. Somehow the elixir of that year, those people, that teacher, those experiences cast a permanent spell. I am forever grateful for that magic.

As he left McPherson, Mr. Ulery gave me the classic recording of Stephen Vincent Benet's "John Brown's Body" with Raymond Massey, Judith Anderson, Tyrone Power. A measure of encouragement and caring far beyond any teacher's ordinary responsibility or salary.

And while this quotation is not from that record, it is vintage Benet and evocative of that debate year:

**Something begins, begins;**
**Starlit and sunlit, something walks abroad, in flesh and spirit**
**and fire. Something is loosed to change the shaken world.**

March 2023

## The "What Was I Thinking" Shoes

Notwithstanding the modest income that kept our family afloat, Mother insisted that we wear good school shoes. They had to fit well; perhaps allow for a bit of growth through the school year; offer arch support; keep my feet from pronating; and be sturdy. Sunday shoes were a bit different—often hand-me-downs from my sister or from cousins. And they could be slip-ons. And summer meant a new pair of the ugliest rubber and canvas sandals you could possibly imagine. In fact, you have to imagine them because even *Google Images* carries no examples.

So school shopping—a once-a-year experience at best—meant a trip to Sweeneys Shoe Store on South Main in McPherson and the attentions of one of the professional salesmen employed there. These were not teenagers, but middle-aged men in dress slacks, long-sleeved shirts and ties. All veterans of the trade. In fact, we had our favorites.

Sweeneys didn't use one of those controversial x-ray machines—fluoroscopes. But each visit did begin by standing on the silver and black metal foot-measuring gizmo. Both feet—data recorded on width and length. If you're interested, the gizmo is called a Brannock Device—named after its creator.

I found each school shoe visit troubling. Early on, I knew that I wouldn't be leaving with cute shoes—the loafers or Mary Janes that other little girls had. But I appreciated Mother's concentrated attention and the shine of a new pair of tie shoes in one form or another.

But then came the pre-high school visit. That momentous transition. And we went to Sweeneys as usual. Other girls were choosing saddle oxfords about then or good penny loafers or just nice white tennis shoes. Even, ignoring winter weather, nice flats. I was closer than I'd ever been to melding Mother's specifications for shoes with current fashion. After all, saddle shoes were sturdy tie shoes. But for reasons lost to me now, my eyes were drawn to a pair of white oxfords. They looked so bright—like they might one-up saddle shoes. They had deep, comfy looking soles. The salesman found my size. They met Mother's preferences. And off I went.

With nurses' shoes. In fact, really well-made nurses' shoes that required constant polishing.

I don't remember how long it took me to realize what a ghastly choice I'd made. I was a dyed-in-the-wool nerd anyway. My clothes all came from Mother's sewing machine. Grades mattered to me. I was likely perceived as a teacher's pet. So I was never going to join the cool crowd. But still...

The shoes were comfortable. I did keep after the polishing. I was embarrassed, but not really depressed. Or angry. I have faint memories of feeling rueful—knowing that I couldn't blame Mother or anyone else. In fact, in a twisted way, I had seen myself as being clever or slightly bold in the choice. But, of course, teenage "look-alike-ness" still mattered—still stung.

I can't remember whether I remedied the situation before my sophomore year. What I can pinpoint is that by the time I was a junior, I'd come into myself in a whole bunch of ways. I'd actually joined the pep club and had the requisite red skirt and vest. I'd become a debater—a good one, in fact. Off to tournaments all around the state. And somewhere toward the end of the year, I decided that I really could beat James Holecek for Student Council President. And did. And somewhere about then Mother must have sanctioned the purchase of loafers. I never owned saddle shoes.

I cannot account for odd memories like this one burbling to the surface. But I am struck by the preferences born of my nurses' shoes episode. For as long as my feet would allow it, I spent serious money and time finding delicate, sexy shoes. And even though my years of walking in heels across Gettysburg's battlefield and Washington D.C.'s marble corridors took a dreadful toll, I still hunt for the most graceful version of an orthopedic, old lady shoe I can find.

November 2022

## The Kitchen

I dream it into three dimensions so many nights—my growing up home. 830 North Ash in McPherson.

The very last time I stepped inside for real—the rooms echoingly empty, I recorded the metallic rasp of the oven door on Mother's ancient Chambers gas range. But the tape never matched my memories. I am left to create the kitchen in words.

I was seven or eight when my dad's employer, the Alliance Insurance Companies, moved from downtown McPherson to a new building on the north edge of the community. That became my dad's excuse to sell our lovely small bungalow for a miniature, mock English Tudor revival house just three blocks from his office. To his eye, our new home spoke more "class" and affluence than we really had. It offered two small but adequate bedrooms. A little den. A small bath created with cast-off marble. An elegant "sunken" half-timbered knotty pine living room with a fireplace. An entry way that served as a dining room. A basement that had once been an apartment, which my dad hoped to use as lodging for our frequent company. A single-car garage. And a diminutive kitchen. Really an unworkable kitchen. One that my dad promised my mother that he'd renovate.

Turns out, in that era before home inspections, the basement beams housed a tribe of termites. Who withstood the waterfalls that cascaded down the cellar walls in every rainstorm. My dad had purchased a real lemon. He was daunted and embarrassed by its problems—ultimately realizing that eliminating the termites and replacing joists was the first, pricey priority.

Fifty years later, both parents gone, the basement still leaked unrelentingly and no kitchen renovation had ever occurred. From the vantage points of middle age, my sister and I knew that Paul and Esther more than had the funds to update the kitchen. But for a pair who always purchased a used car, the potential cost likely seemed exorbitant. I don't think that they grasped where to begin. Or how to live through the process.

Mother managed, soldiered on, put up with that kitchen until she died in the house—a few months beyond her ability to cook. I never heard her complain—although she would look longingly at other kitchens and exclaim over ones designed along a single aisle. Galley kitchens, she called them, with generous cabinets and countertops in easy arm's reach.

Instead, picture a little walk-in closet-like space. With a small bump-out into the garage that previous owners had fashioned to accommodate a stove and a refrigerator—1940s sized. At the north end, a single window overlooked the sink, framed by what-not shelves. A set of yard-long cabinets—uppers and lowers—and yard-long countertops flanked the sink. On the left, the lower space held drawers for silverware and dish towels. Upper shelves held glasses and dishes. On the lower right, a single drawer stored utensils; shelves below held pans and mixing bowls. Baking ingredients occupied the upper shelves.

A chrome table and four chrome/red leatherette chairs sat opposite the stove and refrigerator, pushed up against the wall. The chairs all snugged up around one curved side. That was the kitchen.

Mother wasn't a gourmet cook. She'd majored in home economics, albeit along with English, music, and art. And her take on healthy eating reflected 1930s thinking and economies.

Lunch—at which we all ate even when she had to pick us up from school—was usually bologna or toasted cheese sandwiches or potato or tomato soup with crackers and celery or carrot sticks. Bear in mind that the cheese Mother used in ALL dishes was Velveeta.

Supper (we didn't eat dinner) might be a sausage patty, mashed potatoes, peas, a small pile of iceberg lettuce with half a pear or peach on top. Or sweet corn and pork chops and potatoes fried in bacon grease. Or hamburger in gravy—and the same basic assortment of vegetables and potatoes. And Jell-O. Jell-O appeared often with various fruits suspended inside.

We'd ask Mother to make a big batch of sausage and pinto bean chili for our college friends. Or if the weather was cold and snowy (conducive to "setting" the mush), we'd beg for fried mush topped with sausage gravy. Both seriously economical foods with luscious tastes.

In a world where no teaspoon of food was wasted, I reveled in "restaurant" nights. Mother let us choose among whatever leftovers were available. Or she'd stir those tiny dabs into rice or mashed potatoes and fry up the resulting "cakes."

For many years, my folks rented a locker next to the railroad tracks and in it stored a quarter of a beef or a hog and chickens from the Dresher's farm. Plus vegetables that Mother had raised and blanched before bagging and boxing into the era's freezer containers. Which meant that Mother had to plan meals ahead of time to have secured the main ingredients. Our own refrigerator freezer, of course, was about a foot square. When my folks acquired a second-hand, standalone freezer that lived in our basement, Mother was overjoyed.

Sunday and company meals—often one and the same—were comprised of a rump roast cooked with potatoes, carrots, and onions in the "thermowell" of the Chambers gas range. In essence, a built-in, super-insulated crock pot equivalent. Or fried chicken.

Both roasts and good fried chicken remain favorite meals. The bad news is that I've never learned to duplicate the taste of Mother's chicken. The good news is that now—unlike then—I can recognize parts of a chicken's anatomy other than wings and legs.

In later years, Mother favored Huntington Chicken for big dinners: a combination of shell pasta, chicken from an "old hen," chicken stock, and Velveeta cheese. I was astounded to find a recipe by that name on the Web, although the ingredients now include cream, cream cheese, cheddar, pimento, and butter.

The scritch of the oven opening—that I so wanted to record—occurred at all hours of the day. In the morning, if I heard it from the bedroom, we were having biscuits and gravy—my dad's favorite dish. Throughout the day, the sound translated into cookies or pies or fruit crisps or cakes—all made from scratch. For company dinners, that sound meant that Mother had made her world-class dinner rolls—food for the gods.

In my dreams—in that kitchen—there is always a musty-smelling, much-battered Tupperware container with crispy cookies it. Sitting on top of the toaster on the left-hand counter. As long as Mother could see enough to measure ingredients and not burn herself on the oven, she kept that container filled.

The rest of that counter was given over to the drain board and drain rack—blue rubber, cracked and crazed with age. Plus washed, empty jars: mayonnaise, peanut butter, olive, pimento. Along with washed and dried bread sacks, used sheets of tinfoil or wax paper, and margarine and cottage cheese containers. All, all waiting to corral leftovers.

The right-hand side of the sink offered another blue rubber drain mat for dirty dishes, dish soap, plant fertilizer, a container that held bacon grease, and a second-hand blender. The remaining couple square feet provided Mother's stirring and mixing space—along with a pull-out cutting board.

Meanwhile, the table on which we ate sported a two-tiered bread box; little boxes of pills in current or previous use; more leftover containers; a couple vases; program booklets from various organizations; the city, church, and 4-H phone directories; a small Pyrex dish holding a used tea bag; and the phone.

Plus, the table was Mother's other working space. The only flat surface big enough on which to roll out pie crusts or cool cookies fresh from the oven or hold canning jars after they were filled with boiling peaches or applesauce or plums. All of which had to be cleared away before mealtime.

Mother stood just over five feet tall—delicate in all ways. She took pride, though, in her muscles. The benefit of carrying baskets of wet laundry and fruit up and down the basement stairs. Still, she could barely reach the second tier of cabinet shelves. The sink area could accommodate only one person washing the dishes and one person drying and putting them away. It was a dance we executed after every meal. If we didn't, dirty dishes precluded cooking or baking for the next meal. The space could not accommodate the many generous backsides of women there for company meals—who wanted to help and to visit.

For 4-H fairs, I turned out cookies, banana bread, and biscuits on the table and braved lighting the oven myself, squeaky door and all. That required striking a match—stored in a tiny cubby above the stove along with a big pepper shaker that held salt.

By the standards of any HGTV show, Mother's kitchen was not cute—not even a cozy relic. It didn't function. But Mother did. I treasure and use several kitchen utensils and dishes to remember her by: the flat china bowl that kept pancakes warm as she made more; our sturdy silverware; the Bakelite ladle that spooned chili into our bowls; the little red snapping turtle/clothes pin that displayed uplifting quotations over the sink.

I still dream the kitchen. And its smells and sounds. Often, I'm waiting for Mother to go out to a meeting or shopping, so that I can clean. So that I can replace those stained, cracked rubber drain mats with new ones. So that I can bundle up those glass jars and cottage cheese containers for recycling or the trash. So that—at least in some small way—I can make Mother's life easier—tidier—brighter. And be with her again.

And I still dream the oven door's creak—the sound of Mother in a warm, welcoming, dysfunctional kitchen.

**November 2022**

## Rooms To Let

Maybe not 50 cents. (For those of you who remember Roger Miller's "King of the Road.") But for sure within my budget.

Ada Keifer's red brick Civil War-era house sat at the crook of Baltimore Street on the southern outskirts of Gettysburg. She was a small, wiry, no-nonsense lady in her 70s who ran a rooming house. In 1968, when I got a summer job at Gettysburg National Military Park, Betty, the park secretary, sent me a list of rental options. I secured my space by letter.

Actually I didn't rent a room. I rented part of a bedroom. And another girl I didn't know—who didn't work at the park—rented the other bed. I didn't flinch at that arrangement. Nor at the fact that other families occupied other spaces in the house for a night or two—responding to Ada's "Rooms to Rent" sign in her front window. We all shared the bathroom.

I kept milk in Ada's refrigerator and packets of Instant Breakfast in my room. My daily walk to park headquarters, then the Cyclorama building, took me past the Hall of Presidents and the National Cemetery's Caretaker's house, through the Cemetery and down a long sloping walk to the Park. I repeated the walk in the evening but headed first to a small family diner for a homey entree, two vegetables, and applesauce, always applesauce.

My second summer at Gettysburg, I scored Mrs. Kiefer's sunroom. A hexagon of glass on all but the side that adjoined her living room. Which was then occupied by her sickly sister. I loved my space. I had a sink, a mirror, a bed, a dresser, and roll-down blinds that likely—at night—provided a shadow show to tourists ambling by. During Gettysburg's intensely hot, humid days, the room became almost unbearable. I changed into my girdle, nylons, newly washed white blouse, and green gabardine suit in front of a fan. Slept that way too. But it was all mine.

The bathroom lay beyond the living room and kitchen. I developed the important skill of responding cheerfully to Ada's sister while still moving steadily through the living room toward the lavatory.

If I once knew Mrs. Kiefer's story, I've forgotten it. And am sorry to have been so cavalier. She did not try to "mother" me or strike up a cozy relationship. What I remember most is her creation of two little bright, petunia-filled gardens between her house and the concrete sidewalk. Her faithful daily watering of those with a pitcher. And her weekly weeding and dead-heading—down on her hands and knees in the sun, still in her print housedresses. Her gift of heat-hardy color to the historic town.

**June 2022**

## Antiquated

This little vignette will make no sense unless you remember a time when most houses had just one or two phones, tethered firmly to a wall. When calls occurred more for arrangements than chats. When long distance calls cost serious cash, though the relative charges depended on day of the week and hour of the day.

Yes, virtually the dark ages.

I was likely ten. The phone rang. And though I often did not answer it, I did that time. And a man said, "Want to meet me for a movie, little girl?" I hung up. Scared; grossed out. Like I'd done something wrong. My childhood had been laced with admonitions against talking to strange men. And I had an uncle who made that training seem wise.

So when the phone rang again, I let my mother answer it.

I had just hung up on Grandpa Pyle calling from Geneva, Iowa. My mother's father.

Grandpa and Grandma Pyle—Milton and Myrtle—were, in fact, the approachable grandparents. They raised their eight children on a farm—in the early days—rented. My mother Esther was the third oldest and the smallest and scrappiest of the bunch. When Norma Jean—the surprise baby—came along in 1933, I think their circumstances had improved. And by the time I knew Grandpa and Grandma, they'd moved into the tiny town of Geneva with a lot large enough to raise an enormous garden.

Geneva was a hot steamy nine hours or so from McPherson—in those years. We'd usually visit in August. Which meant that their garden was at its most exuberant. We feasted on corn on the cob and green beans, squash and tomatoes. Fat black and red raspberries topped our bowls of Cheerios for breakfast. Wonderful except for the hefty seeds buried in berries before hybrids tamed that annoyance.

We'd make afternoon trips to visit other relatives or my mother's school friends. Play with cousins. Pick the vegetables we were approved to harvest. Read Grandpa and Grandma's Grit newspaper and farm magazines. At night, Sonja and I were given the back bedroom/sewing room/storage space. The room's most distinctive furnishing was a black and white cowhide rug. I spent a good deal of emotional energy puzzling over the cow and her life and her sacrifice. The rug seemed pretty superfluous to me—and a questionable kind of feature.

Of course the house wasn't air conditioned. And Iowa's humidity exceeded that of our Kansas home by several degrees of misery. So we went to bed and lay spread eagled with no top sheet. Hoping for a slight breeze.

Grandpa and Grandma's pictures match my memories. Word had it that Grandpa had had a temper and he still rather expected the world to accommodate his whims. But he was also the tease. The twinkle in his eyes real. Grandma Pyle was less jolly, but had her own wry wit and wisdom. And no illusions about Grandpa. Her voice was scratchy, always on the edge of giving out. Which seemed reasonable for a farm wife who'd raised eight children and superintended gardening and housekeeping and cooking and farmyard chores without any of what we consider modern conveniences. Who wouldn't have worn through their vocal chords!

In 1952, Grandpa and Grandma celebrated their 50th wedding anniversary. Milton had been 22 and Myrtle 17 when they married. To the best of my memory, all their children, most of the spouses and grandchildren gathered in Geneva. And in a custom which seems just as antiquated as that early phone call, grandchildren put on a kind of talent show. My sister gave a dramatic reading—memorized with nuanced voices and gestures. I fought through sheer terror to play a very simple version of "Teddy Bear's Picnic" on the piano. Sonja may have sung along too.

Rather like my contemplation of that cowhide, I loved to picture those teddy bears. And their picnic in some magical cool forest that in no way resembled Kansas or Iowa. Why wouldn't we attend?

*If you go down in the woods today, you'd better not go alone.*
*It's lovely down in the woods today, but safer to stay at home.*
*For every bear that ever there was*
*Will gather there for certain because*
*Today's the day the teddy bears have their picnic.* *

I spent today with the youngest four of my grandchildren, Izzy and Ella and David and Charlie Ann. And drove the 100 miles home wondering now how they would remember me. I'm Grandmom to them. Probably too serious for their tastes. Maybe recollected for weird gifts, for asking irrelevant questions, for needing their help to pull me out of their squishy sofa, for hearing only about a third of what they say. But really, I haven't a clue whether or how I'll live in their memories. What quirks will sift through their lives and this century? My life being as antiquated to them as a Bakelite phone seems to me now.

**June 2022**

* *"The Teddy Bears' Picnic" melody is by American composer John Walter Bratton, written in 1907; lyrics were added by Irish songwriter Jimmy Kennedy in 1932.*

## Imprints

At the edge of sleep,

Just as Simon's paw reaches under the covers for my cheek,

I wake at home. The corner of North Ash and Earl, in McPherson.

The brick bungalow that my dad thought more stylish than the frame one on Marlin.

In that flicker of a moment, I am ten again—and look across the hallway to see if my parents are up; listen for water running in the bathroom next door and the rasp of the Chambers Range oven door from the kitchen. Mother might be baking biscuits.

It's a quarter century since I've been there. More like 50 years since that was home.

But the imprint of that layout defines my waking subconscious. And in no way matches my current floorplan.

I must consciously and with grief remind myself that Mother has been gone for almost 30 years. That I am old—and living in this peaceful condo alone, save for Simon, the white specter. And while no one is waiting to stop by the bedroom door with a chirpy and often unwelcome "rise and shine," all is still well.

I enjoy a handful of other less-encompassing, less fraught imprints:

The tastes of Mother's fried chicken and fresh green beans and canned peaches and birthday angel food cake with crackly seven-minute frosting. No equivalents have ever captured her flavors.

The summer evening chorus of cicadas. I dreamed it one night this week, the rhythmic rise and fall buzz saws, and went looking for the outgrown shells the locust shed. Childhood trinkets.

The Community Hall's scent on Kiwanis Pancake Day. The steamy elixir of batter and bacon and syrup on a cold March Saturday. The essence of Carnegie Library—books, paper, linoleum, pee. Peanuts from Woolworths' roaster—hot and fragrant in my hands as we walked them home to Mother.

The emotional time-machine that graces my bed. The quilt Mother pieced from dresses she sewed: beauty, embarrassment, sexiness, self-importance.

I have lived a life many times more glorious than I ever imagined in that front bedroom on Ash. Homes and work, Bob, Dave and his daughters, landscapes and friends. Branded, too, in my psyche.

So why am I returning to that place? Why am I lingering over the experiences that are behind me—that register so sweetly in my soul? The view beyond my keyboard tonight is come-hither-magazine stunning. I will never run out of books that take my breath and heart away. I am surprised every day by the understanding and compassion of my friends. So, why—

Maybe, maybe in these world-gone-crazy days, I long for the refuge of that first nest. For the days when I was responsible only for schoolwork, dusting on Saturday morning, setting the table.

Maybe in some elemental way, I am reliving the anticipation I felt then. That small-town, mid-century Kansas belief that the world was good and that I could be and do to the limits of my daydreams.

Maybe it is simply the grief of growing old—of saying goodbye to more than we welcome into our lives.

Maybe it is the joyful intricacies of our beings and brains—the ones scientists have only begun to understand. Or maybe the very intricacies we fear. Whimsy at work in the stream of time.

**May 2022**

## Friday Afternoons in the Chief Historian's Office

He was the kindest man I've known: scholar, gentleman, Lutheran, dad, husband, boss, Chief Historian of the National Park Service (NPS). Although Dr. Harry Pfanz had too little confidence in himself, his political instincts were spot on. If his heart lay in research and writing, he was still the perfect, practical guy to represent the business of history for the National Park Service. Blessed with much common sense, perspective, an understanding of historical context and the agency. But full of contradictions. A nervous nelly. Flustered by higher-ups. Modest, self-effacing—self-deprecating, in fact. And yet he knew his mind. And could speak it. Well-dressed but not natty. Forever on the edge of chauvinism, though never into misogyny. And aware of his foibles in the arena of feminism. According to Harry, Mrs. Pfanz, Letitia, reminded him often.

In fact, I better stop right here and tell you about the Monday when Harry came into work and admitted to being flummoxed. (Remember, we're talking mid-70s here.) His church had just "invited" women to be ushers. All well and good, Harry said, except that they disrupted the symmetry and order that occurred when two male ushers walked up the aisle side by side to return the collection plates to the altar. What once had seemed orchestrated and smooth now involved one smaller party bobbing along on high heels next

to a taller, smooth-gaited man. He knew that we would give him grief for weeks to come. If nothing else, I admired his willingness to share the perspectives that he knew he had to relinquish.

I met Dr. Pfanz while I was still at Gettysburg. A Civil War historian, he came to help narrate a film that some office in NPS was crafting—maybe a training film about one of the battlefield farm houses. We talked during the down time that such filming often involves. Once back to his office, he called and encouraged me to apply for a vacant position in his Washington D.C. NPS central office. I moved into a lovely little Arlington, Virginia apartment just as Richard Nixon was moving out of the White House—August 1974.

I was one of two staff historians, Barry Mackintosh being the other. We were lodged on the first floor of the ponderous Interior Building. Part of a grouping that included historians, archaeologists, and architectural historians. We were the conscience of NPS in the care of its historic and prehistoric resources.

We read truckloads of planning documents and environmental impact statements and prepared comments on the adequacy of their intentions regarding cultural resources. We crafted briefing documents about places being proposed as new cultural parks. We wrote Congressional testimony and public speeches for NPS big wigs. Our office taught brand-new rangers the whys and wherefores of historic preservation laws. Which entailed trips to Harpers Ferry, West Virginia, and the Grand Canyon training centers. We rode in on our white horses to parks in conflict with the public or among staff on how historic resources should be treated.

In fact, the position came with astonishing opportunities. I took two familiarization trips (maybe read "junkets") by myself. One from D.C. through a host of parks on the Eastern Seaboard, finishing up in St. Augustine, Florida. That jaunt included not just a host of Civil War and southern historical sites, but a night in a Holiday Inn honeymoon suite—the last room I could find in Savannah. My second educational venture began after I taught a class at the Grand Canyon and then visited all the NPS Southwest mission sites south to the Mexican border, cross country to Fort Bowie (an Indian Wars/Apache site in Arizona's Chiricahua Mountains ), on across New Mexico to Fort Davis in Texas, and concluding at LBJ's ranch. Hmmm. As I write this, I'm wondering why I ever left the job.

Single-purpose trips included an outing to see Carl Sandburg's home just as it came into the Park Service. Yosemite Valley during a fight over the significance of historic tent camps. The Adams home in Boston. NPS was also long on conferences and confabs, and when those involved historic resources one or more of us flew in.

But back to Harry and the office. It dazzled with wonderful fellow feeling. We played pranks regularly on each other. Harry's archrival in the Civil War history business was a fellow named Ed Bearss. Ed lived in the far reaches of D.C. suburbs so would bring his suitcase in to the office on days he was flying out. With Harry's cautious approval, Barry and I once "salted" his suitcase with female lingerie and perfume. Harry was known to nod off during warm afternoons. Barry and I chose such a moment to "borrow" Harry's suit jacket and stitch the sleeves shut. And then arranged for the secretary to the deputy director for cultural programs to call Harry up just at the end of the day. Harry was left trying to jab his arms into the suit jacket required for any third-floor appearance. A Scot by temperament and heritage, Barry ate exactly the same sandwich every day. Really, every day. And, to my current chagrin, I once substituted fake cheese for the real slice. Barry didn't notice right away.

Fridays then. We answered a lot of odd incoming mail from citizens all across the country who wished and hoped for new parks, who took issue with interpretive information, who were sure that an overlooked relative had been a central figure at a historic site. We answered quickly and kindly. But—we saved some of those incoming letters in a special file for Friday afternoons. Not every Friday, but periodically, Harry would unearth the more improbable requests and encourage us to write the answers we really wanted to give.

As best I remember, there was the fellow somewhere in Florida who had built a kind-of-sort-of colonial-era fort from scratch, he told us, and thought it would be the perfect addition to NPS. No, it wasn't on the site of an earlier fort. No, he really hadn't researched the design. But he knew. Couldn't we see it? Our official letter, of course, cited the criteria for historic parks and monuments. Their authenticity. Their provable historic presence. Their role in pivotal moments in the history of the Nation. Jargon, of course, to someone who lived in his own version of history.

On Fridays, with such a letter in hand, we let loose. "You, daft sir, have a make-believe resource. The National Park Service is never going to touch it with a ten-foot pole. Write your Congressman as many times as you want; the answer will be the same. Even your Congressman knows better. You could, of course, approach Walt Disney." You get the idea.

Or, more hauntingly, we carried on an extended real correspondence with a gentleman who wanted us to designate a park that would commemorate all the children lost in school bus accidents. He had a site in mind. The issue was personal for him. Our real letters had to address the fact that the Park Service rarely created such memorials. And even when such existed, the site needed to be of national significance. And how do you tell a grieving parent that?

Our Friday version was far less tongue-in-cheek than the one we crafted for a make-believe fort. There are only so many ways to say that we were sorry. But we did address the difficulties that would follow if a park were to be created. What kind of orientation film would someone craft: scenes of crashes occurring; pictures of children in body bags; stories of bus drivers with drinking habits?

Just before the end of the day, we would read each other our alternate answers. The weekend would be upon us as the Interior Building emptied. And our colleagues headed to buses and ride shares. In fact, Harry was always in a lather about meeting his carpool compatriots on time. The rules of the road meant that if he was late, they would go on without him.

I meant what I said mid-essay. Why did I leave that job!

**April 2022**

## The Incomparable Old Red Barn

I've lived for 40 years in breathtaking landscapes. Where, from our deck at The Land, the Backbone of the World—40 miles of the Rocky Mountains—stretches into infinity. Where night after night, my home range—the Big Belts—turns gold and pink and purple in reflected sunsets. Where the earth's curves unravel along quiet highways. Where—barring fires—the clear air and clouds magnify our limitless sky. I live in a land of hyperbole.

But last night, heading into sleep, I traveled back to Washington D.C. and walked in memory into the offices I occupied there. The massive, 1930s Interior Building. A flimsy, nondescript multi-story 60s building on L Street—on the edge of changing neighborhoods way past all the fancy lobbyists' digs. And then, and then, into the Pension Building. And I couldn't breathe or sleep or stop the longing to be there. I knew what my fingers would be trying to describe today.

Designed by General Montgomery C. Meigs, Quartermaster of the U.S. Army, the entire block-encompassing, fireproof building took shape between 1881and 1887. A home for the Pension Bureau and a monument to those who fought and died and won the Civil War. Bohemian-born sculptor Caspar Buberl created a terra cotta frieze depicting Union military units and action. It banded the entire enormous

red brick Italianate Renaissance Revival building. Even with the spectacular frieze, the Pension Building's detractors applied the sobriquet: the old red barn.

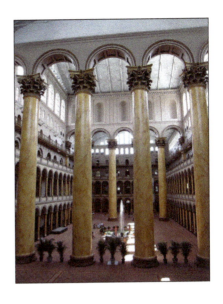

Those folks must not have stepped inside. Where they would have been greeted by an atrium—the Great Hall—rising 75 feet before being topped by a tall clerestory structure. Huge Corinthian columns defined the space. Three floors of interconnecting offices lined the atrium's perimeter reached by arcaded galleries. Creating light-filled working spaces. And healthy ones—courtesy of Meigs' ingenious circulation system.

By 1978, when I moved in along with other historic preservation folks, the building had been lightly occupied by an assortment of federal agencies for almost 50 years. Sometimes empty; sometimes a whisker away from demolition. The office spaces were shabby. The fountain that should have played under the soaring central clerestory windows was quiet.

Long before the cut-and-paste architecture of the middle and late twentieth century, ancients understood that settings influence our behavior. Deliberative bodies tackle their work with greater care and wisdom when situated in elegant, beautiful spaces. We view the Oval Office as demanding serious state craft. (We've been fiercely disappointed in both examples recently.) Every religion in the world counts on lavish architecture and ornament to attract and impress followers. To suggest that deities are best summoned and honored in glorious places.

General Meigs didn't quite aspire to a temple of worship. But he designed his big red barn with reverential intent. First, to honor the two million men who kept the Union whole. And to allow the personnel responsible for paying veterans their pensions to work in a bright, airy, functional space. No more Bob Cratchits in dim smoky offices, but respected civil servants doing the Nation's important work.

For two years, I got to walk into that echoing space every morning. From my World War II garden apartment on the edge of Alexandria, I took a bus to the Pentagon. And transferred there to the Metro that delivered me to the Judiciary Square stop. I read the *Washington Post* along the way. At the top of the Metro escalator, I had only to turn around and walk across the street into the unassuming front door. Then past the empty fountain and angle northwest across the yawning courtyard to the office I shared with Bill Lebovich. To a desk and lamp that turned my tiny place in the building's history into a pool of light.

Walking that courtyard or running errands along the balcony. Or heading to the restroom, I felt as if I passed through a portal in time. Surrounded by the spirits of the men and women the building honored. Held in a column of light and a host of lives past. Akin to being under a night sky defined only by stars and their time-traveling brilliance. Only and oddly more ethereal, more personal. Literally and figuratively, I stood straighter; thought more creatively; felt more alive. Hyperbole made manifest. Familiarity blunted that mystical sensation a bit, but never altogether. And now two thousand miles away, remembering, I catch my breath all over again.

By the late 70s, during President Carter's redrawing of the Interior Department, things began to change. In 1980, Congress authorized a new museum to celebrate the nation's architectural and engineering skills and history. The Pension Building was to be its home. The perfect marriage of space and purpose. I visited the old red barn, the National Building Museum, just once in its new role. The fountain burbled. The atrium buzzed with families, lost tourists, children's games. As it should have. I was glad to have visited and I understood the gift I'd been given to be in that dome of light and history alone—in quiet.

So here's my question tonight: do I want to revisit D.C., take the

Metro to Judiciary Square, and walk into the Pension Building. Or, now, in this time in my life, am I better served by the transcendent memory of being THERE, at work, when it was mine.

March 2022

## The Late Baby – The Surprise Kid

It was always going to be tricky—adopting the State Historic Preservation Office into the Montana Historical Society's established family. But needed. For a decade the Parks Division of the Department of Fish and Game had given the young program a chancy home. Managing it with guys who wanted to be game wardens. Hiring a Wyoming shyster to write a preservation plan. Skimming off federal grant money for state parks.

So when federal preservation overseers came to scrutinize Montana's preservation program, they called a halt to the negligence that the SHPO (pronounced "ship-o") had experienced.

Move it to the Montana Historical Society (MHS), they recommended. Place it with its philosophical kin, its siblings who will understand its purpose and its professional requirements.

The legislature did just that in 1977. But no part of the adoption went smoothly. Turns out those siblings were reluctant to share their parent organization. And, as the Preservation Office grew, SHPO staff, with some regularity, questioned whether they belonged.

The Montana Historical Society boasts early origins: first such society of its kind west of the Mississippi River. Born in gold camp Bannack in 1865, the Society became a state agency in 1891, just after Montana achieved statehood. In the early 1950s, it acquired its own building and most of its current functions.

In the 30 years prior to SHPO's arrival, the Society had achieved some serious maturity. Exhibits; archives, library, and museum storage; reading rooms; an award-winning magazine; and offices occupied the modern building. The Society enjoyed the adulation of scholars, visitors, and art aficionados who gobbled up Custer and Charlie Russell stories. Into that comfortable arrangement, the Preservation Office arrived—young, unsure of its place—or the manners it might need—or even how best to tackle Montana perceptions.

You see, Montanans readily understood that Indian War battlefields and Copper King mansions and Virginia City might be historically significant. But really, were shabby homestead remnants or Boulder Hot Springs's crumbling edifice significant? Weren't there serious dangers to designating a historic property? And did the Society want to upset the apple cart of good relationships with power companies and subdivision developers just to send some archaeologist out to find ubiquitous tipi rings?

I arrived in 1980 in the Preservation Office's early Society years. Forty-one years later, in 15 of which I served as State Historic Preservation Officer and another ten in education and administration, my perceptions of whether SHPO belonged in the Society hold steady. Of course! Of course, even in the face of tempting and not altogether irrelevant arguments to the contrary. Here's why.

SHPO does exactly, precisely what the Museum and Library and Archives do. We (I still think of myself there—in that office) encourage the preservation of historic buildings, sites, and places of significance to Montanans. Period. Archivists and curators encourage the preservation of artifacts and documents and books and artwork of significance to Montanans. Period.

The Museum, Archives, and Library have the authority and the space to acquire and hold some of the materials they focus on. But they cannot acquire every single artifact or document that's important. No such facility could be big enough. The SHPO is not empowered to own property. Nor could or should it "move" important buildings and places into one warehouse as a form of preservation.

So, all Society programs, to a greater or lesser extent, rely on spreading information and enthusiasm to preserve in place, on site, in the right contexts—Montana's various historically significant items and resources. Ownership is only a question of more or less. The goal is the same: get Montanans to value the physical remnants and information that help us understand and appreciate our past.

The similarities end, though, when it comes to rules and funding. The national historic preservation movement emerged in the face of massive 1950s, federally funded development:  interstate highways demolished whole neighborhoods; housing programs did the same. Preservationists realized that the country was losing—not the obvious landmarks—but the historic fabric of towns and cities and the pre-historic sites and farms of the country. Hence, the National Historic Preservation Act of 1966 required federal agencies to evaluate and at least consider the significance of resources that would be harmed by their actions. And the same law created a network of SHPOs to help identify sites and buildings that might be important to their communities.

So, federal law, federal money, and federal programs constituted the foundation on which Montana's SHPO was built. Therein lay the biggest challenges to the Society's enthusiastic adoption of this new program. As well as SHPO's periodic battles with its new home.

Other Society programs, even with shared motives and advocacy for their work, weren't based on federal regulations. So, whereas, the Preservation Office confronted red-faced mining agents bellowing about why the Forest Service had to consider %%**## sites in the permit area, the Archives and Museum programs faced no similar regulation-based fury. Where would such fury end, those programs wondered.*

The federal money awarded to the SHPO had different ramifications. When it was plentiful in the early 1980s, other programs envied us. SHPO received state funds too—half and half—for staff and office support. Sheer luxury.

Then in the late 1980s when its revenue plummeted, the state began whacking away at all agency budgets. Because the SHPO had federal money, along with state funds, the Society could sacrifice SHPO state dollars without eliminating staff. The SHPO was "invited" to fill in behind the losses with their federal funds. The feds accepted in-kind match rather than actual cash. The Society continued to nibble away at our state dollars. The SHPO staff felt rightly and unduly put upon.

In that mindset, SHPO staff began to dream about what it might be like to be their very own entity. Some SHPOs were just that. But, at least from where I sat, that way was folly. The Society provided a host of administrative services, kept us legal when contracting or hiring, lobbied for us, and, frankly, stood as a buffer against political and business whims. Not a single director sold us out to development interests. They did what it took to keep the agency whole—even if not always with the vigor we craved. Even when we were welcomed more for our money than our mission, we weren't facing hurricane force winds alone. We were part of a generally beloved family.

The fact of the matter is that we were good for each other. Because SHPO worked with property owners and state and federal agency staff all across Montana, we had a statewide presence. Before other programs did. Over time, we got to know local historical societies and county commissioners and architects. All too often seen as the Helena Historical Society, MHS could piggyback—if they chose—on our statewide work. Consider our National Register of Historic Places interpretive sign program. For just $25, owners of listed properties can get a lovely, permanent marker that credits MHS for the sign and the listing.

Significantly before the rest of the agency understood how critical it was, SHPO established strong and warm relationships with tribal culture committees and First Peoples preservation advocates.

Though slow to be seen as such, the information about Montana's history captured in National Register of Historic Places nominations and in broad historic and archaeological surveys is invaluable to researchers. Likewise, the library and archives' historic newspapers and photographs and original documents are critical fodder for people writing Register nominations. More symbiosis.

Finally, as the Society began to expand its K-12 education efforts statewide, SHPO's National Register materials, contacts, and philosophies have become the basis for heritage education lessons.

I still like the analogy of a family with a surprise baby—a-late-in-life arriving kid. Siblings rarely get along sweetly and enthusiastically all the time—however and whenever they arrive. We fight to establish who Mom and Dad love best. But, when the chips are down and sometimes when we've grown up a bit more, we gain the wisdom to understand that we flourish as a family.

*State antiquities regulations mimic some—though not all—federal preservation regulations.

March 2022

## Off to an Inauspicious Start

I'd spent that 1980 April morning interviewing. The Montana Historical Society's Preservation Office program manager job was up for grabs. Notwithstanding the fact that I'd just snagged a great position in the National Park Service's Washington Interpretive Bureau, I applied. I wanted an "I'll show-you-the-world-is-my-oyster" adventure. Professional and daring one-upmanship over the people who'd broken my heart.

So I'd flown out from D.C. and was staying at Jorgenson's—Helena's 1960s "political" motel. It was close to the Capitol and the Historical Society, had a heavily-used, deeply smoky bar, and a restaurant long on family favorites served by skinny, permed spinsters. I'd enjoyed a full country breakfast and likely stank of cigarettes.

I walked to the Society for my 9:00 am interview, past Helena's ugly shopping mall. Along the way, at an intersection, I mistook a handicapped-accessible, audible "walk" beep for some exotic

Montana bird.

The Director had assembled every last Society program manager and what must have been a couple spares for the interview. We were installed around an antique dining table covered with glass, sitting on matching straight-backed, wickedly uncomfortable chairs. Not kosher museum practice. One overturned coffee that seeped under the glass and the table would have sported stains!

The interview seemed not to have been orchestrated with agreed-upon questions. It felt like a carnival shooting gallery and lasted until noon. Whereupon we all got up and went to another vintage motel restaurant for lunch. I always hate having to eat in a group, but especially when I'm nervous. Plus, Brian Cockhill, the Archives program manager, kicked off conversation by asking what winter sports I liked. And without thinking, I said "none."

The truth of the matter was that I'd thought more about what I might get away from in Washington D.C. than where I might be headed. And what it would be like. I'd worked for the central National Register of Historic Places office; understood what federal law required state historic preservation officers to do; knew that Montana's program was so befuddled and youthful as to require special assistance from Washington. I knew, too, that the previous preservation officer had departed abruptly after threatening to resign if her demands weren't met—and they weren't. The office secretary joined her in protest.

What I didn't know much about, at all, barring basic geography and history, was Montana. Her size, her temperament, her economy, her topography, her politics, her population—much less her stock of historic resources. You'd think the interview might have gone in that direction. But apparently my competition, a favorite of the Society's press editor, was a candidate from Florida. I had, at least, crossed a tiny corner of the state on my way to school in Oregon. And I'd reviewed one or two Montana National Register nominations in my central NPS office work.

In the afternoon, Library Director Bob Clark took me around to Society's offices for awkward introductions. After a stop in the bowels of the Archives, he turned me loose on the edge of Territory Junction, a basement installation of phony 1880s storefronts serving as artifact displays. I'd later learn that the "Junction" was the most visited of the Society's exhibits. But in my stupor that day, I wasn't sure whether MHS employees would pop out in period dress.

The Preservation Office lay around the corner and behind the row of territorial stores. Enclosed on two sides by glass, either a fishbowl or the innards of Territory Junction. The lights were off, though I spotted a person inside. I stepped in and introduced myself to the architectural historian and was met with her deadpan face and brusque response. The room held a table, a couple desks, a row of file cabinets, a door to an even darker room—all situated on a grimy yellow and white shag carpet. I couldn't figure out what more to say, or what to ask except about other staff. The architect was just out. The archaeologist was up on the Hi-Line at his family's ranch. I kept moving.

Once in a while I've turned down jobs for which I've interviewed, but not as often as I should have (remind me to tell you about my last working gig). Mostly, once I've invested in applying for a position, I become attached to succeeding. As happened here. I was vacationing with friends in Arizona when the Society director called and made the offer. Within a month, I'd cashed out my National Park Service retirement, packed, put my Alexandria, Virginia, condominium on the market, found tranquilizers for Sooty Cat's plane ride, contracted with a moving company, and flown back to Helena.

You may remember that I purchased a stick shift Toyota within a day of arriving and swooned over Helena's June lilac profusion. Plus, after lurching up and down Broadway and working my first day, I arrived back to my new apartment to find my belongings gone. A cleaning crew had emptied out the wrong unit—although they did leave Sooty. I was told I'd find the property manager in the Securities

Building bar. I hustled over. Only to fall ass-over-teakettle from the threshold onto the bar's sunken floor.

And at work, I began to absorb the office's degree of disorder. The dirty shag carpet stank of dog. I needed to hire a secretary; locate a desk for myself; find functioning typewriters (a problem which entailed a marginally successful trip to state surplus property); encourage the archaeologist who was still waiting up at his family ranch for a favorable report about me to return; and joggle the architect into appearing regularly.

For all that I'd worked in offices for more than a decade, I'd never started from scratch: to figure out how to order supplies; to learn and then revamp a filing system; to master new phone and mail and procurement procedures; to build a rolodex of contacts. Then, more important than just having names and numbers on file, to begin the process of fitting people and their niche into a workable context: federal agency, state agency, district manager, forest archaeologist, community leader, local historical society doyenne. And beyond that, to suss out their particular powers, fears, skills, and angles. To get a handle on Montana's geography and the kind of prehistoric and historic resources that reflected our history.

Life within the agency was complicated too. Until two years prior, the Preservation Office had been housed within the state Fish and Game Department. Where it was seen as a cash cow for state parks rather than having a statewide mission. So we were still new to the Historical Society and viewed with deep skepticism. We traded in controversy and threatened to politicize the gentle world of Western scholars and museum curators. Our office received precious federal grant money, as other departments did not. The press editor remained disgruntled that I'd been hired over his candidate. The exhibit fabricator, whose carpentry shop lay across from our door, pined for the voluptuous secretary who'd just departed and lobbied for a similar replacement. And though I was slow to spot all his serious liabilities, I began to see the Society Director as the wimpy, manipulative fellow he was.

Then, there was the doorbell. A Society, of course, protects its archives and artifacts from danger. The basement door to the building was just a few yards away from our office. Security consisted of a doorbell outside that solid door which we—with no information about or glimpse of the visitor—answered by pushing a corresponding door release. Heck of a system.

Three weeks after I arrived and had mastered the stick shift's psyche, the Hill County Historical Society invited me to speak at their summer meeting. I don't remember how they knew I even existed or had taken the job. I don't remember what I was to present. I do remember looking at the map and noting a three-hour drive to Havre, partly interstate. Easy, I thought. I'll go up in the afternoon. The program ends at eight. With June's long daylight, I can be home by midnight without too much time in the dark.

I learned several things on that trip: that the drive was drop dead gorgeous; that attention from Helena mattered a good deal in far flung corners of the state; that community members were eager to talk about their town, their projects, their historic sites, and so sought leisurely conversation before and after the program. My decision to drive home the same night was both faux paus and dangerous. If I stayed over, I could have seen more, appreciated their history more. Still, I carried on with my plan. And somewhere about midnight, in the long curves and hills of the Missouri River corridor between Great Falls and Helena, I saw a huge snowy owl flying beside me.

Reality or hallucination? I've never been sure. Then and now, I trust in the owl's symbolism—though every culture has their own take on the appearance of that nighttime messenger. Surely not an omen of death. I chose to embrace another culture's belief instead: that he represented wisdom and intuition and independent thinking, especially during this new adventure. How could I not?

**March 2022**

## A Preservation Office Pastiche

I'd write a more fulsome history of my 15 years as Montana's State Historic Preservation Officer, if I could remember them.

That alone is a puzzle. How is it that the defining position of my adult life is, in memory, so devoid of details? I can—without missing a beat—launch into a spiel about why historic resources are important. Or describe my philosophy for dealing with arrogant, intractable developers. Or explain why the Preservation Office belongs in the Montana Historical Society. But query me about any given year or many different projects, and I'll likely refer you to my friends Milo McLeod and Janene Caywood, whose memories are second to none.

I'm also short on explanations for that fuzzy recall. I had a lot going on: courting, marriage, North Fork weekends, caring for Dave's parents down the street and mine long distance, Dave's health, my surgeries, Emily and Amanda with us summers, then Amanda year around. Staff changes, two office moves, three directors. But all of that's adulthood. Everything really that most people experience. So, I'm perplexed.

What I can summon, though, are moments. The strobe lights of time and memory as they wheel around to catch a person, a moment, an event, a reaction. Followed by the lingering shadows of feeling.

Why not start at the end! My mother died early in January, 1995. The legislature was in session. I'd made a very bad hiring decision before I'd headed to Kansas. We were in the thick of defending the importance of the Little Rockies, an island mountain range culturally significant to the Gros Ventre and Assiniboine. The mountains faced another round of open pit mining. I'd already entertained a visit from the crude bully, Pegasus Gold's hit man. He'd made the purpose of his visit clear when he pulled his chair as close to me as he could get—knees almost touching, his face in mine. We were to change our position, declare the Little Rockies of no cultural import. I didn't back down.

I'll tell you about the paper route elsewhere. Suffice it to say that by April, I was weary, overwhelmed. And the Society Director Brian

Cockhill invited me over to his office to tell me that Pegasus Gold and other mining and power companies were blackmailing the Society. They threatened to defund the entire agency—all of its museum and archive and library programs (and such was their power) unless I was removed as Preservation Officer.

Bless Brian for his creativity and compassion, and a certain respect for the work our office accomplished. He found a way for us to have our cake and eat it too. The Education Officer slot was vacant and I transferred to that. The State Archaeologist became the Preservation Officer and continued to support the significance of the Little Rockies. The Society kept its funding.

Better moments from earlier. We were uncommonly fortunate to hire Lon Johnson as our Historic Architect early in 1981. Soft-spoken, skilled, dead-on in his judgements. But when Lon left for another position, finding a credentialed architect who loved and knew old buildings proved daunting. Ultimately, I hired Herb Dawson, an Oklahoma good-ole-boy who'd been Wyoming's State Historic Preservation Architect. With that decision made, I headed out on a three-week summer vacation to The Land. And, for the life of me, couldn't remember Herb's name. What I knew was that Herb was a larger-than-life, Harley-riding, gun-owning character. My amnesia seemed Freudian. Especially when Herb arrived—post vacation— roaring up on his Hog and throwing open the office's double doors. Dodge City or the Preservation Office. Herb brought his own idiosyncrasies to the office, but he knew his stuff and could work with developers. The leathers didn't hurt.

Mostly my colleagues were a dazzling group of professionals. And creative. During another longish summer North Fork vacation (sans phone), I began to get mail from the staff. Photos showing them climbing into state cars, stowing their luggage. A letter on office stationery described their decision to take a cross-state trip. They explained how they had handed off care of my cat and forwarded the office phone. That was followed by post cards from various unusual locations. All a hoax, of course, but the effort they invested in creating the "story" was so clever that—as they intended—I couldn't be altogether sure. We reveled in great camaraderie for a long while.

Including the winter of 1989 when temperatures never reached zero and our cars died one by one. We crafted changing circuits around Helena to pick up staff without functioning vehicles. A process that got more interesting after a train crash took out all Helena's power.

There was the night I rolled into a wooden, double bunk at primitive Camp Maiden in the Judith Mountains, with a young Amanda. And realized that we had both spread our sleeping bags over a heavy sprinkling of mice turds. But the event changed everything about the relationship between conventional preservation processes and Montana's First People. Dave Schwab, one of our archaeologists, had family ties to the Confederated Salish and Kootenai. Dave had worked patiently, largely by himself, to bridge the process gap between archaeological and tribal ways of knowing—the difference between digging and measuring as opposed to history spoken through generations. And it was Dave who suggested that we invite Native cultural ambassadors and Montana's many archaeologists to a special event. We would host. Provide good food. Gather informally, eschewing motel conference rooms and written agendas. Be somewhere folks could stay in cabins or vans or tipis. And we would talk... and eat... and thank the Creator, and learn to know each other. Our children could play together. Camp Maiden became a tradition. It changed our commitment to First Peoples and properties of traditional cultural value. For sure it changed me.

In 1991, facing a mastectomy, I was showered with get-well cards from around Montana, good friends as well as prickly adversaries. And Salish tribal elder Tony Incashola called to tell me that he and the other elders would be asking for blessings for my recovery and good health. His was the face and voice I remembered as I rolled into the operating room—along with Dave's.

I gave a lot of presentations in those 15 years: encouraging, explanatory, admonishing. Depending on the audience, I'd use props to hold their interest: a beloved stuffed animal from my college years and my dad's ingeniously designed family syrup pitcher to help explain National Register criteria. A doll house to talk about how historic buildings could be "read" and described. I'd tell the story of my preservation conversion at Gettysburg—the power of standing on the places where history happened. And on the occasion of the Cascade County Historical Society's annual awards banquet, I was to celebrate their successes. When invited, I learned that the organization's members usually dressed in historic period clothing and enjoyed seeing each other's choices. I was encouraged to join them. Which meant that after much internal debate, I bought a girdle and squished myself into my mother's 1950s church dress. It featured big aqua and brown flowers, a side zipper, and an asymmetrical neckline with a fabric bouquet. In fact, I didn't try to don the dress until I'd reached Meadowlark Country Club and changed out of comfortable clothing into that number. Only to realize, as the group gathered for dinner, that no one else was dressed in historic outfits.

Speaking, meeting, explaining meant a whole lot of travel. In fact, I'm so struck now by the time-saving possibilities that Zoom would have offered then. Well, and lifesaving. I have distinct memories of gliding ever so slowly but surely off I-90 just outside Missoula in freezing rain. Dave Schwab was my unlucky passenger but chivalrous enough to tromp through feet-high barrow pit snow, climb a fence, and find a phone. Then there was the icy night coming back from Red Lodge in our brand new family Toyota 4-Runner. I did a one-eighty on top of Bozeman Pass and could see semis coming up at right angles behind me. I managed to turn around.

I walked out of only one meeting in my tenure. We were in Missoula and the owner of a cultural resource consulting firm, long on making the most money he could by catering to his developer clients, told me that we (hear I) were crazy to believe in the significance of some historic site (I wish I could remember what). That we didn't know anything about Montana history. No arguing on the merits. Just on our judgment.

Montanans mostly embraced National Register of Historic Places designation for elegant homes, one room schools, main streets studded with turn-of-the century commercial buildings. But we had a far harder time convincing people that the resources most distinctive to Montana and our particular human past were significant. In part because those very vernacular, organic resources too often got in the way of land management and development. Think historic bridges, roads for heaven's sake, ranch headquarters with all the attendant corrals and shops and bunkhouses. Trails and railroads. Cultural landscapes—whole chunks of discrete unchanged valleys. Irrigation districts. Tipi rings, stone drive lines. But there was a moment in a meeting with Forest Service regional office staff that I felt the tide shifting. I'd been explaining the significance of backcountry fire lookouts and ranger stations to an annoyed crowd. This was their history. A green uniformed man at the edge of the room spoke up. He allowed as he was a baby boomer and he didn't know about the other guys in the room, but when he retired he doubted that he'd want to pitch a tent at the end of a day's hike. He'd rather, he said, sleep off the ground and cook his breakfast on a wood stove. Maybe turning those Forest Service back country structures into rental cabins wasn't such a bad idea. His perspective helped to launch one of the singularly most popular land management preservation efforts still in place. Ever so slowly but surely the importance of other vernacular resources gained acceptance.

Other flickers of light, of memory:

The time I was so hornswaggled by Dave that I forgot to send out legal notices for our quarterly State Preservation Review Board Meeting. Nothing like having to call nine professionals around the state to confess.

The annual last minute, frantic, whirlwind of a time to gather the statistics for both our year-end report and our application to the National Park Service.

The year that the evil, slimy director demanded that I bargain for management against Dave who was bargaining for the employee union.

The heart-to-hearts I needed to have with every single secretary to promote filing.

My fraught and inadequate search for a house that would fit a new archaeologist arriving from California with his family and children and a rabbit and a dog. Bless the whole family for their bravery!

The arrival of the heartthrob of a consulting archaeologist when I could hear sighs of longing in the office space behind me. Or the tongue-tied agency archaeologists there to meet with either of our two gorgeous female archaeologists, one of whom had been Miss Montana.

The coup de grace to my departure from the Preservation Office in 1995 came when the preservation community honored me during their biennial ceremony. Smooth-talking, chameleon Governor Marc Racicot (a sweeter friend to industry than he let on) took a moment as he started to hand me the award, leaned in, smiled for the camera, and, knowing full well why I was leaving the Preservation Office, had the audacity to whisper: "Everybody has a shelf life."

March 2022

## Wrangling With Teenagers

They were looking for a fight—those mining company executives and disdainful forest supervisors. The subdivision developers, the highway engineers, the power company managers, and, of course, the university presidents. Many were poised—if not eager—to intimidate, to call in political favors, to ignore us—the annoying and surely irrelevant Preservation Office historians and archaeologists that we were.

They were teenage bullies. They wanted to do what they damned well pleased. And they anticipated—maybe hoped—that we would be unreasonable, demanding parents.

It took me awhile to figure that out. To learn the dynamics of a place where property rights, a long history of deferring to big industry, and a strong distaste for regulations and women ruled. Nonetheless, where a certain affinity for our scenery and our pioneers mitigated those uglier influences. I had to learn how to take both into account.

Preservation laws do not mandate that any agency or any private interest must save a National Register eligible property. Like the National Environmental Protection Act, historic preservation laws are **process** laws—not outcome laws. The law directs agencies or their permittees to **evaluate** historic properties **and consider** the effect of a project on them. And to **look for** ways to lessen or mitigate harm to such historic resources. That's all. **No entity is required** to save significant properties, regardless of other consequences.

Tricky.

But back to those teenagers. Likely an unconscious reaction, though not necessarily: they wanted to be told what to do. They wanted me or my staff to demand that they save the lithic scatter or the ranger's cabin or the abandoned schoolhouse. They tried hard to construe whatever I said or wrote as a command. And if or when I made such a decree, I became the foil, the villain, the unreasonable impediment to progress, economic development, job creation.

Then, the agencies and developers could make historic preservation a political fight. Or at least a messy one.

Hence, the somewhat obvious approach I arrived at over time.

I would remind the agencies or companies that wanted a fight that they could do whatever they chose—after they'd gone through the required procedures. But neither the law—nor I—had the power to force one solution over another.

That strategy required matter-of-factness and confidence. I couldn't be smug or flippant—even in my mind.

Within the office, my easy leap to that game plan wasn't always popular. Some staff felt it to be an inappropriate concession. Keep those bullies in fear for a while, they wished. Act as if we had legal muscle.

The longer I served in the Preservation Office, the more the strategy felt right. What I said was absolutely true. Posturing as if I had power would backfire. The honest approach often took the wind—the arguments—out of folks. We got down to the real issues sooner.

But more important, a thoughtful process was—in fact—the very ethic that preservation advocates and I sought—always—whenever a historic or prehistoric property was at risk. Recognize historic value—and consider it. Give it some decent thought. See if you-we-the public could have a bit of our cake and eat it too: a subdivision road that skirts a prehistoric site; a logging project done in winter instead of summer when snow buffers artifacts; honest consideration for building reuse rather than demolition.

There weren't always work-arounds to achieve preservation. But once in a while there were. So, a serious effort to consider a project's impact and some alternatives to damage was itself a victory. A very real public good.

As it is, often, for teenagers. We want our kids in those dicey years to think about consequences.

Amazingly, that freedom was often enough. A little time invested. A little consideration applied. And the better angels of those agencies or people sometimes appeared. Not always. But sometimes. History and scenery occasionally trumped profit or expediency.

Even if those improved perspectives occurred after one more round of protest. Like teenagers, sometimes the agencies wriggled and whined in the face of having to make grown-up decisions.

The right process did take time and money. Hiring archaeologists or historians. Waiting for evaluation and treatment options. And once more, the teenage analogy applied. The more an agency wept and wailed and postponed the legally required process—the longer it would take to accomplish their project. Their choice.

It was all in my attitude or that of the staff. It paid to speak the truth graciously, comfortably. To do so without being defensive or taking the discussion personally. "Of course, you can upgrade that highway. You just need your archaeologist to survey the area and help you through some planning steps."

That was then.

Now, in 2022, I'd place no bets at all. None. On whether my old-fashioned appeal to process would work. The teenage bullies of my working years seem to have become self-satisfied, smug-countenanced adults. Told that they could do what they want after taking cultural values into consideration, they would ignore the last "after" and do what they wanted sooner. The other half of the Montana paradox I came to know—that respect for our history and the majesty of landscape and habitats appears to have diminished. And selfish, uneducated, brutish teenagers appear to be in charge. Showing the rest of us just how much of the state they can destroy if they choose.

**March 2022**

## Powerless – Unmanageable

The Brethren of my youth defined themselves by "no's."

No smoking, no drinking, no gambling, no taking the Lord's name in vain.

No attachment to worldly goods or fun that might lead to sex before marriage.

We were only years beyond no dancing.

Thankfully that stricture had been struck.

We were to follow Christ's example—and words,

Although that rule raised more questions than it answered.

Jesus loved sinners. He had nothing at all against wine. The Gospels did not demonize joy and play and fun. Fishing was encouraged.

Which made it easy, in graduate school, to accept a glass of spirits from Dr. Govan's wife, Jane.

Though when I purchased my own bottle to sample the night before my orals, I tripped on a curb coming home from the grocery store. And broke the bottle of wine in my grocery bag. God was, it seemed, reminding me of the rules.

That morality lesson evaporated the next decade: Gettysburg and D.C. came with the lovely rituals of cocktail hours. With trusted friends. Limits understood. The sweet balance between sober and silly. The marvel of—just for a small while—feeling freer, less obligated, less prudish, less responsible. Rarely if ever edging toward chaotic; dangerous; deadly; malignant.

Which meant that when I hit Montana, I was not ready for the drinking that defines the West.

Which meant, at first, Dave's six-pack of Michelob seemed innocent, easy.

Until, of course, it wasn't.

Until I was so far out of my element that I became the crazy companion. Governed by terror and panic. Distrust. Disgust.

There were no elegant cocktail conversations.

Just wild swings of anger and maudlin affection.

And I thought—as I'd spent my life thinking: that this wasn't real. That love should conquer all. That I couldn't go on. That I couldn't **not** go on. That there was—and then there wasn't—a way out. That there had to be something I could DO! NOW!

We live in a state where drunk driving is the norm. We are the land of Big Skies and Big Drinks. And a reputation as the place where real cowboys can hold their liquor and their loves at the same time. And where our highways sport the white crosses of carnage. Where we rank third in the nation in suicides and drunk driving fatalities. Where the price we pay for our liquid bravado is death.

And the price I paid for applying the force of my will and the absurdities of circular thinking bathed in fear and anger—was its own hysteria. Kansas girl, D.C. minor civil servant running right up against the disease of alcoholism—animated by the West's pernicious legends—didn't fare so well. And certainly didn't change or help Dave.

I required the educated wisdom of a counselor and the even more apt, understanding, and lived experiences of Al-Anon friends to survive. And finally to thrive.

I had to learn a batch of realities that turn out to be useful—critical in fact—in absolutely every other moment in life: that by force of will we never change another person; that we are utterly powerless over others' addictions; that we can only forever be responsible for our own actions; that loving people by letting them live the consequences of their choices is the only love we have to offer. That letting go of our infernal wish to change and control others may birth pure magic.

In 1910, tee-totaling temperance Kansas crusader Carrie Nation swept through Montana and realized few converts here. Dave wrote one of his *Montana Campfire Tales* about her. And by the time he did, he had largely banished six packs and vodka bottles. A great job at the Historical Society, published writing, speaking tours, daughters embedded in our lives, and the elixir of freedom from all the pain and pressure he'd tried to control (courtesy again of a counselor) gave him a lease on life that didn't require alcohol.

But that's his story.

Mine was learning the difference between irrational clinging and letting go; between paranoia and peace; between control and caring. And relearning that, or trying to—again and again. Up the North Fork. When Dave traveled. When his health crashed. Yesterday. Today.

**April 2022**

## The Paper Route

I was just home from watching my 87-year-old mother die.

For her, that meant the blessing of peace after months of fear and unease. The cruel additives to her illness.

For me, that meant the agony of watching light leave her eyes.

She'd fought her whole life to be old enough, brave enough, busy enough, happy enough, caring enough to make her own way in the world.

Fiercely ignoring a few realities that might have stifled her spirit, but didn't.

Living on her own terms.

And that included her determined walk to the post office and back again to mail the many cards and letters she wrote, the caring she sent out daily into the world. Her breath of fresh air. Her exercise.

Her final gift was the donation of her body to medical research.

I came home to Helena—in awe of her living, chastened by my own.

I am again now as I gather these words.

But in that moment, my eye caught our newspaper's advertisement for a paper carrier in our neighborhood.

Why not, I thought. Prescribed exercise before work. A strategy that would keep my feet to the fire of walking.

Dave had the good grace to ask if I was nuts. But left it at that.

The job was mine.

By design, my first day was a Saturday. Not by design, following an ice storm. Even the grass was slick. What I thought would be 20 minutes of walking took two hours and involved several treks back home where—in good light—I could try to match house numbers with reality. Oh shit, that apartment building had a door at the back. Dammit, that garage was a house.

Then came Sunday and while the footing was better, I hadn't reckoned on manhandling the grocery supplements and funnies and car dealership inserts.

But I wouldn't give up right away.

I hung on long enough to go through four months of collecting what was owed, little book of payment tickets in hand.

I hung on long enough to go from a brightening sky through the time change that sent me back to dark again.

I hung on long enough to develop a weariness that no amount of napping could shake.

I hung on until a young girl, out for an early morning walk in Helena, was kidnapped and killed in our end of town.

Dave's only final request was that I keep the sturdy canvas apron—pockets front and back—that came with the route. Perfect for repair jobs at The Land.

Now, I cannot piece my thinking together. Or imagine Dave's real dismay and disbelief—and the annoyances of my 5:00 am alarm.

I only know that we all face grief and remembering differently.

March 2022

## Fish Out of Water

If I had any doubts, the jig was up the afternoon that our Regional Park Managers quarterly meeting morphed into a Missouri River float trip. We had assembled in moderately rustic facilities at the Beartooth Wildlife Management Area. I'd bunked in a simple cabin and found my way to the SST (shorthand for Sweet Smelling Toilet in FS or FWP lingo, which is shorthand for the U.S. Forest Service and Montana

Fish, Wildlife, and Parks). I'd contributed to the discussion and hadn't embarrassed myself with city clothes. But when I realized that our final afternoon would be spent rafting, I wanted to slink home. But we had carpooled.

The first serious difficulty appeared as crew leaders picked passengers for each raft—and I was clearly going to be chosen last. The float was not meant to be educational or scenic. It was a much anticipated and traditional water war. Crew leaders wanted aggression and strength—so as to "man" the water cannon already placed in each raft.

About the third bend in the Missouri, already soaked, I got to re-membering that the Montana Historical Society was advertising for an Operations Chief.

Two years prior, I'd left a perfectly wonderful post as the Society's Education Officer. Fish, Wildlife, and Parks—after decades of casual care for their historic and prehistoric resources—had created a visitor services/cultural resource position. Good on them, I thought. And ap-plied. Thinking that my previous experience would prove just the ticket.

In fact, it proved just the ticket to being hired but not for maneuver-ing well, given the agency's temperament and behaviors. FWP needed a person to hike up hill and down dale, jaw with park managers about camp hosts and chronic wasting disease, handle the mechanics of his-toric site documentation, and periodically stand on some rock and yell "NO." I brought theory and words and procedures.

Which meant that too many of my days were devoted to skimming park planning documents; writing comments that would be ignored; taking familiarization trips; attending the agency's blizzard of train-ing sessions, meetings, and trendy self-evaluation seminars; reviewing contracts; speaking occasionally to this group or that about why his-toric resources were important.

I worked with some very good people. Mostly men, of course. Well-intentioned. Cordial. Trying to do right by some incredibly significant sites and buildings: Lewis and Clark's Three Forks of the Missouri and Traveler's Rest; the ghost town of Bannack; Crow Chief Plenty Coups' house. But still always out of their primary element.

Familiarization forays were magical: all the dinosaur-laden stone gargoyles of Makoshika; the architectural delicacies of Elkhorn's standing structures; the scenic breadth of the Madison Buffalo Jump; the twists and rolls of Belt Creek as it wound its way through Sluice Boxes mining remnants.

In fact, my introduction to Sluice Boxes occurred on a day-long raft trip—spring cleanup and knapweed patrol. All of which went well, until the Parks employee—somewhat woolly-headed anyway—accidentally steered us into a big rock. I catapulted out of the raft. The incident became: park manager drowns central office woman. A foreshadowing of things to come.

Central office employees in FWP suffered the same stigma as most headquarters employees do. We made a questionable amount of money. We were mostly talk and title. We had no line authority over day-in-day-out decisions. With the exception of capital projects—construction, significant remodeling, site development—activities that needed major funding. There we had some authority.

Which brought me to the First Peoples' Buffalo Jump State Park (at the time called Ulm Pishkun). FWP had owned only the upper plateau across which bison were driven toward a cliff edge. Through a series of small marvels, the agency had just acquired acreage near the bottom of the jump—the artifact-rich processing area—and enough money and additional land to build a small visitor center.

While FWP could manage basic construction contracts, staff had little experience creating exhibits. Hence, they'd thrown a boatload of money to a big, out-of-state interpretive design firm—which employed no historians or archaeologists or Native people.

As I started to get my FWP legs, Ken Soderberg, the visitor services guru, realized how generic, empty, and misdirected the fancy firm's ideas were for the exhibits. Fortunately, only in preliminary form.

I'd already found a kindred spirit in Ken. He had solid credentials in park management, didn't shy away from water sports, and came from a really creative family—skilled in music and theater and wordsmithing. In other words, Ken was already a bridge between my background and that of the park managers.

I more than agreed with Ken's assessment of the design firm's empty thinking. And we gathered the courage to break the contract and begin our own planning.

We first had to determine what the exhibit's goals should be. And after some serious research, Ken and I determined that our task was **not just** to showcase the mechanics or timelines of the jump or the "products" buffalo offered. But to give visitors a way to understand the cultural framework, the spiritual practice that native peoples employed in hunting buffalo. The calling—the summoning—of a being so magnificent, so powerful, so needed that each part of the ritual was sacred.

We then hunted for and found Krys Holmes whose understanding and writing skills matched those goals. I culled Dave's shelves and the Society library for sources that gave us detailed descriptions of how the buffalo and buffalo jumps featured in the lives of Plains natives. I'd been to the Canadian Head-Smashed-In Buffalo Jump World Heritage Site and could reach out to staff there. I knew First Nation's cultural leaders here in Montana—critical voices and memories.

I valued researching in traditional sources and less conventional ones. To the extent I could, I worked to step outside the twentieth century and see our landscape and its resources through very different cultural eyes. The trips between Helena and Ulm were their own immersions in beauty. Ultimately, Krys and Ken and I zeroed in on the words and images that seemed worthy of the place and the people.

The Visitor Center's dedication occurred after that water war on the Missouri. I did not attend. Instead, I had applied and was hired for that Historical Society position.

But reports of the event came back to me. The ceremony included a moment—unscripted—when the crowd—agency staff, community leaders, tribal participants, ranchers—circled the building. And reached for each other's hands as First Nations elders offered blessings for the buffalo and for the Center's mission to create an understanding of Plains people.

~ ~ ~

Turns out I'd leapt from the proverbial frying pan into a scorching fire. Or from a turbulent river into a typhoon. That's another essay. Meanwhile, FWP found their way to hiring an archaeologist whose skills and heart matched the opportunities and problems that the defined the agency. Still, maybe I was there at the right time.

January 2022

## The Montana Heritage Project

The Meagher County Poor Farm sits on the western edge of White Sulphur Springs, Montana. You turn off beside the once-grand old Ringling house and follow a winding gravel road until you come to what, at first glance, might be an enormous farmhouse. Lots of windows, porches listing a bit, angles—having grown like Topsy and then slumped while struggling to find a new purpose.

You can say that about the whole town of White Sulphur. Never really a booming place, its hot stinky sulphur springs drew nineteenth century miners. Logging and wood processing brought a small wave of mid-twentieth century busyness. It's a county seat with a diminutive courthouse and more bars than other businesses on Main. Kept on life support now by recreationists, a summer festival, and some folks who hope that a controversial new mine will bring jobs.

It was the kind of small Montana town whose children Liz Claiborne and husband Art Ortenberg worried about. The designer-businesswoman and her husband had two Montana retreats. One of either side of the Continental Divide. They were here often enough to get a feel for the state, its boom and bust history. And to see that few small, rural towns held onto their high school graduates. What a shame, they thought. Worldly travelers that they were, the Ortenbergs understood that small town living in this high plains geography had a rich history and much to recommend it still.

Along with the Librarian of Congress, James Billington, a personal friend, the Ortenberg's hatched a proposal that became the Montana Heritage Project. Fleshed out by its first director, Michael Umphrey, Folklife Director Alan Jabbour, and Montana Historical Society staff.

The Project was to engage small town high school students in primary source community research history. To set them on a course of conducting oral histories; delving into old newspapers, county records, historic photographs, city directories, Sanborn Fire Insurance company maps. And to do so, with a theme or research question in mind. Students were then to share what they had learned with their communities—in booklets, walking tours, essays; public programs; exhibits; assistance to local museums. In other words, to give the fruit of their research back to the community in some format.

The thinking behind the Project was that such deep dives into local history would inevitably introduce teenagers to colorful stories, community characters, whole chapters of their towns' past that were no longer evident or had been forgotten. Those findings and the community enthusiasm generated would—the Ortenbergs thought—let young people see their homes in new and attractive lights.

It worked.

In terms of logistics, small high schools—led by one or two teachers—applied for acceptance into the Project and funds that would help with a bit of travel, printing, exhibit creation, a community night

event. On the Project's dollar, teachers attended a winter gathering and a summer week-long symposium with well-known authors and historians. Teachers received financial assistance for travel and further study. Each spring all the involved schools brought students to a statewide gathering that showcased the students' work. Students and teachers from one school each year were given the opportunity to travel to Washington D.C. and present their work in person to the Librarian of Congress.

I first participated in the Project sporadically, from other positions at the Society and the Parks Division. From his post in the Historical Society library, Dave always helped students and teachers find primary source materials in the Society's holdings. And tutored them on where local resources could be found. Later, for another five years, I got to work directly for the Project—one of three staff people.

Project Director Mike Umphrey's thinking fostered much of the Project's success. He understood that most teachers are so harried that they needed extra time and compensation to take on leadership and creativity outside their required duties. That they would thrive when they had time and resources to be inspired. He knew that English teachers would have more latitude than history teachers who were bound to US History curriculum. He understood the power of great photographs taken throughout the school year—and ways to share those—so that students and teachers could see themselves at work, being successful.

All three of us working for the Project made a point to visit schools often—especially community history events. And to help locate the resources that a given class needed.

So, over the course of the Project's active decade, Simms students interviewed Vietnam vets in their area to hear how their war experience influenced their current lives. That included the blustery high school vice principal who broke down in tears during the interview. Harlowton students researched how the electrified Milwaukee Railroad and its demise influenced their town. They tracked that story in railroad worker interviews and in historic building patterns. Townsend students read literature relevant to their community's history, interviewed old timers, and then drew parallels between Townsend's evolution and that portrayed in literature. Corvallis students examined the impact of wildfire on their community. Dillon kids investigated one room schools throughout the county. Roundup scholars created interpretive museum labels for family artifacts. Chester High School project students put on a fashion show: girls in their mother's or grandmother's wedding dresses; boys wearing their father's or grandfather's military uniforms. Art and photography teachers pitched in. And so schools created a dozen variations on these activities and themes.

You will have seen this coming: White Sulphur Springs students researched the history of the Meagher County Poor Farm. They identified employees who worked at the Farm in the late 1940s and early 1950s and interviewed them. They found the Farm's yellowed, brittle register of occupants—dating back to the 19th century—in the county courthouse and conducted an analysis of what brought individuals to that facility. They photographed and documented the Farm. And of course, while doing those tasks, learned about the poverty and loneliness of ranch workers; the waves of illness that moved through Montana communities in the early part of the 20th century; and attitudes within their town about Poor Farm residents.

Dave and I found community programs especially powerful. Students usually set up displays and haltingly, proudly gave verbal reports. Music teachers were sometimes recruited to lead a school chorus in old time songs. Refreshments were important. As were generous public thanks to the elders who had been interviewed or shared antiques or photos. Such programs were rare celebratory evenings for many communities—and students. Free of political controversy. An opportunity for a struggling little town to celebrate itself. For older residents to see their memories and experiences valued.

The Project ended in 2004—the Ortenbergs, Liz especially, were in ill health. They had been happiest when they could influence the Project's course and attend Project events. Truth be told, they loved meddling a bit, second guessing teachers and staff periodically. The Project was less compelling to them when they could not "participate."

We didn't try to assess the Project's results numerically. No graphs or charts. No tracking students to see who returned from college to their communities. Nor did the funders really expect that. The feedback we received from teachers and students during the Project's active decade was specific and joyful. It boiled down to the magic of doing work and learning skills and information that mattered. Not just memorizing textbook quizzes.

I had been enthralled especially by that Chester wedding gown/uniform review. The students had not just found costumes in the back of closets. They had interviewed their relatives and studied each item's historical context. One wedding dress was a pink two-piece suit worn to elope in a neighboring town. One had been made of parachute silk—an economical choice brought back by a returning World War II soldier. I like to think that when some of those students married or entered the military that they recalled their parents' and grandparents' stories—and saw themselves in that great but changing fashion show of time and circumstance.

*A special hats-off to all the Montana Heritage Project teachers. Their time and creativity and caring made the Project what it was.*

May 2022

## The Last Library

Don't count them out. Or think them made redundant by Google. They are damn pure magic. Portals into time travel. Archetypes of standing stone circles, temples, pantheons of all the gods we've worshipped over time. If we let them, they prise the spears and guns from our hands and replace them with information and empathy. With history, science, music, the novels and essays and poems we've crafted to explain life to each other. They are built on the wondrous belief that humans have the honor and obligation to save what we know—and offer it to each other.

I love libraries.

~ ~ ~

In 1960, I began my working life at the McPherson Public Library as a high school freshman. Forty cents an hour. Flossie, Lavilla, and Jessie my supervisors and advocates. A classic historic Carnegie building; children's books in the half-basement, adult fiction and nonfiction up above.

Fifty-five years later, after a string of post-Historical Society retirement jobettes, I saw an ad for a part-time library aide. Ten hours a week, $11 an hour, at the Clancy Library. I didn't know that Clancy had a library. Evening and weekend hours—an attraction. It was January and every damned early-dark afternoon sent me howling to bad TV. And wouldn't it just be too perfect to draw my working career full circle. I did a little reconnaissance, drove the lovely 13 miles down to a historic red schoolhouse. I turned my imagination loose; invested some serious energy in the application; and got an interview. I love libraries.

My expectations slid closer to reality when I interviewed. We talked in a battered, chilly former classroom/meeting space. A 1960's addition housed the library rather than the historic building. The spaces were dingy, dark. The floors uneven, badly carpeted. The bathroom had served small children; stall doors didn't lock. In fact, this building shared the primal scent of pee with McPherson's Carnegie edifice. I didn't know whether I'd interviewed well and wasn't sure what outcome I wanted.

So, of course, I was offered the job—although the librarian, whom we'll call Linda for the purposes of this essay, did ask twice if I REALLY wanted to take the position. You may remember that such offers are my undoing. All too quickly, I'm invested in "yes."

I honored the yes for ten months—for most of 2015. I resigned truthfully and officially because I could no longer read book titles or call numbers. Macular degeneration had begun its creep across my retinas. But my heart had been struggling with THIS library for some time.

It served the mountainous, northern end of Jefferson County—just south of Helena. An adjunct to a somewhat larger facility in the county seat 20 miles south. Our patrons included doctors and lawyers who'd found scenic perches for million-dollar homes; middle-class state employees in quasi-subdivisions; and a fair share of almost-off-the-grid families and bachelors. The town of Clancy itself housed a good-sized K-8 school; two churches; a small-town cinder-block post office; a bar called Chubby's; another eatery with ever-changing ownership; and a scattering of old and new houses. It had once existed to serve hard-rock miners.

I found much to appreciate. We did an impressive, steady business. Linda had massaged our hours of business to match patron needs with available funds. Retirees, job applicants, and students put our three computers to good use. Folks who couldn't afford the newspaper or wanted company stopped by. The area lacked cable or hi-speed Internet, so we offered an enormous collection of DVDs. And were a frequent stop for parents on their way home from work to gather weekend entertainment. The library had a sizeable collection of character cake tins that could be checked out just like books. A clever offering, it seemed to me. Books on CD were popular with commuters. An older woman with developmental disabilities spent time with us and treasured several children's books. We hosted a summer reading program—albeit fueled not by the rewards of reading but by toys and gadgets.

Regular adult books ran to newish popular fiction, especially rom-coms and mystery series. Craft books and back-to-the-land guides held pride of place in nonfiction. In children's nonfiction, cartoon and joke books saw the most activity. We hosted a story hour with the library's small, but current picture book selection. In older kid's fiction, we held both old favorites like Nancy Drew and newer fantasy novels. Linda maintained a paperback collection in the outside corridor—grab and go service.

I checked books in and out and shelved them; found requested items. I took more pride than I should have in remembering the Dewey Decimal system and having the alphabet tattooed in my brain. By spells, with a list from Linda's in hand, we culled books deemed too unpopular to warrant their space on the shelves. We pulled and boxed books destined for yet another smaller branch facility several miles away. Toward the end of my tenure, I began helping with the simplest cataloguing.

I loved learning about the interlibrary loan system: the networking that shuffled requested volumes among libraries—thus vastly extending each facility's holdings. In-state loans were free to patrons; we charged for long distance. The State Library contracted with a medical supply company to carry loaned books to and fro as they traveled Montana on medical business. And, for one remote community, local librarians themselves had arranged for beer truck drivers to make deliveries. Beer being the commodity sure to get delivered even in Montana winters. Everything about interlibrary loan services gladdened my heart—except the archaic, hand-written tracking system that our librarian had devised.

I needed longer than I should have to learn the library's computer system for checking books in and out. It wasn't hard, but I found myself flustered when patrons or other staff watched. Names were forever on the tip of my tongue as opposed to where I could say them out loud. I seemed often to be one slight misstep away from trouble when I opened or closed. Or when I retrieved books from the book drop. I've never had an easy relationship with lockers and keys.

Truth be told, practical realities contributed to my interest in leaving the library. Standing on poorly carpeted concrete caught up with my hips and back. Getting up and down from bottom shelves was difficult. Ten hours a week didn't seem like they should interrupt the rest of my life. But those hours occurred over four days, required a change of clothes and the assembly of a mid-shift snack, and rarely ended on time. The space could be plenty hot or plenty cold. I'd come home too knackered to sleep. Thirteen miles was easy except in snow. And, after many years of managing offices, I didn't take to being supervised or to some of the supervisor's practices.

The librarian did not, in fact, welcome the woman with developmental disabilities. Or get along with the person who managed the little museum housed in the actual red schoolhouse. Or, for that matter, with the library board. She devoted 80 or more hours a week to the library—sweetly martyred when any of us proposed alternatives. And because she was so keen to expend her entire life for the library (all of holiday weekends, for instance), her sacrifices became odd leverages. Stealthy demonstrations of her rectitude. Further damning in my eyes, Linda's politics dictated a steady stream of dicey purchases—far right conservative diatribes, confidently displayed. Without buying the work of liberal writers. Or moderates.

In the end, though, it was all about the classics. And what their treatment demonstrated. Linda stoutly refused to shelve classics (think *Little Women* or *Treasure Island* or *Grapes of Wrath* or *Moby Dick*) where they belonged among all the other books. Most were, instead, shoved into a storage cupboard set apart from the library. They didn't appear in our computerized catalog. Patrons—usually students—were left to approach us at the desk and ask if we had Alcott or Stevenson or Steinbeck. And that required us to leave the library unattended, dash down the hall, unlock a cupboard, and rummage among a heap of volumes not even alphabetized. More recent significant books (think Wendell Berry's novels, for instance) that weren't judged as classics just got culled.

I queried and pushed Linda farther than she liked. Her reasoning seemed to be grounded in numbers. If she counted the classics as part of our collection, the library's per-volume assessment from the State Library increased—and decreased the number of more popular books we could purchase. To which my inner voice still rose up and shouted: "They're the classics!" To placate me, Linda mused about moving the classics back into the library space and housing them on a shelf so high someone would need a stool to scan them. Literally beyond reach.

Barring the possibilities offered by the interlibrary loan system—functional but cumbersome as it was—we were a library built wholly on what was popular. And especially on what was popular with our patrons. Where once I felt that libraries threw a rainbow of diverse and fascinating material into the world, I found that our little library whirled in a downward spiral. Since the common denominator for survival on our shelves was popularity (or the librarian's political leanings)—that common denominator itself became skinnier, more contracted.

Years ago, in my Washington D.C. summer as a guinea pig, I'd toured the Library of Congress. And grew goose bumps as I peered down into the reading room's astonishing beauty and heard the guide describe the Library's mission: to hold EVERY book published in the U.S. and many more beyond. And anyone—anyone—was welcome to research in the Library. That experience threw into greater relief the narrowness of spirit, the poverty of intention with which our little place functioned.

And is this all moot? In the six years since I left the little library have Google and Kindle supplanted our need for or interest in public libraries? That was the prediction. The answer is: not in the least. Humans have a stubborn attachment to the tactile experience of books; the reassurance of paper; the convenience of leafing through a tome and settling on what we want. Which means that libraries remain pertinent, singular. For those of us who are intense readers, we crave browsing—skimming along shelves, stopping at an odd title, perusing the books that neighbor the one we thought we wanted. And therein the poverty of my little library.

No library can acquire and hold everything—though philosophers in the ancient city of Alexandria tried for a time in the 200s BC. And every librarian makes difficult choices, with active circulation being one criterion for a collection. But excellent libraries seek to afford their community the best of humanity, or at least a sampling of that, as captured in media of all sorts. Small or large, libraries—librarians— can choose to shape their holdings with curiosity, with the breadth of their own reading. With delight in offering their community of readers and searchers more than the mediocrity of what's fashionable.

Helena itself is still served by such a place. Then, remember Kay, my art teacher family friend from Minnesota? In the golden years of her retirement, Kay volunteered to shelve books in Hallock, Minnesota's tiny library. The library was part of a regional system managed by a person who shared Linda's views on culling anything that didn't circulate much. Kay's greater contribution to the library was to check out endangered classics—of all vintages—often so that the computerized system marked their popularity. The back seat of her car held those treasures just long enough to demonstrate their importance. I love libraries and those that fuel their great dreams.

March 2022

## Amen

It seems the notices come weekly now

As one classmate after another dies.

The news relayed by a faithful Bullpup

Who's lived his life in McPherson. Or hers.

A pillar now of the community,

A Kiwanian, a Lion, a Chamber of Commerce board member,

A business owner whose home-town success was not foretold

By his high school hijinks.

And then the tributes arrive. Mostly from jocks

For a fellow jock.

And I remember the padded shoulders and the camaraderie,

The impish smiles. The silent brotherly shoves.

And I return to our small concrete-benched gym or to a brisk fall night

Laced with the scent of a friend's plate-sized white homecoming mum,

The red pipe cleaner "M" its stamen.*

There was only one boy from whom I craved a mum—or a date,

Or the gift of a locker-side conversation.

And he died this week.

As usual, the obit and photo shared with those of us living.

But so far, without the tributes.

Dick played football—same as the others.

But hustled home afterwards to farm chores.

His smile eternally open, genuine, shared.

His capacity for wise and kind asides enormous.

Forever free of the call to be cool.

At first glance, I didn't recognize Dick at the one reunion I attended.

Nor did he know me.

I was, though, star struck by the serene beauty of his wife.

Ann's gracious openness. Her class.

Dick had found and married someone

Who shared his gentle goodness.

I was glad for them, and jealous, and reassured

By the wisdom of my unanswered crush.

By the grace of their friendship.

I was puzzled only by their evangelical fervor.

To what is a Kansas farm boy born again

When he already knows the sweet sacraments of gold wheat,

Steady wind, sunflowers, a blue sky stretching to infinity, dressed with whipped cream thunderclouds?

Though, if such pentecostal faith gave Dick and Ann the peace they needed this week, I am saying a heartfelt amen.

*I thought every community knew about Homecoming mums with pipe cleaner letters. Rendered in school colors. Turns out that may have been more specific to McPherson than I realized. Trust me, it was a thing!*

**March 2022**

## Now, This Day

You and I would agree, I think, that heaven such as the one anticipated by "true believers" does not exist.

That your Plains Indians heroes and the armies that killed them do not reside on gold-lined streets or answer to either a benevolent or judgmental deity.

But that the many dead whose lives drained out on our nineteenth-century high plains land are still sensed by, still known in spectral form to their native descendants. Or, if they died in blue with their boots on, alternately saluted in spirit by a handful of those in thrall to the U.S. military's false and wicked glory.

Truth be told I suspect you didn't dwell too much on what came after this life. Your life. There were sturdy genes in your family. You'd lived long enough to begin to feel the edges of immortality.

And you never laid your keyboard to rest.

You have long since forgotten or refashioned our time together. Such is reality. Not unlike what we all do with every bit of the history we purport to know. It was you who put DeVoto in my hands!*

Still, now, this day, in whatever ephemeral space your spirit occupies, I would wish you these gifts:

Your hearing restored. So that you could be returned to the trills of "Garry Owen;" the drums and shouted commands of Trooping the Color; the soaring pathos of Gounod's "Faust;" the "Mikado's" three little maids; the rollicking chorus of "Bringing in the Sheaves." To the comfortable conversations with historians and park superintendents and admirers whose questions and praise and misdeeds suffused your years.

Energy and sure-footedness. Your mornings launched with the exhilaration of an early run—days anticipated, paragraphs crafted in your head.

Sweet and peaceful cocktail hours. That sunset-radiant time you savored at the end of a week's work—negotiation, explanation, inspiration.

Perhaps lazy afternoon chats with the very people whose lives you examined and explored. Pulling from memory the questions that archives never answered. Custer himself and Elizabeth; Geronimo; Billy the Kid; Sitting Bull; a barracks full of soldiers somewhere in the West; a campfire coterie of natives whose memories and words have eluded historians.

The heady, joyful tension of getting up to speak.

Just maybe a gray cat to curl up at your feet. Maybe not.

Color and pageantry.

And time alone. Quiet time. The grace and breadth of eternity.

*"Biography is the wrong field for the mystical, and for the wishful, the tender-minded, the hopeful, and the passionate. It enforces an unremitting skepticism—toward its materials, toward the subject, most of all toward the biographer... His job is not dramatic; it is only to discover evidence and analyze it. And all the evidence he can find is the least satisfactory kind, documentary evidence, which is among the most treacherous phenomena in a malevolent world. With Luck he will be certain of the dates of his subject's birth and marriage and death, the names of his wife and children, a limited number of things he did and offices he held and trades he practiced and places he visited and manuscript pages he wrote, people he praised or attacked, and some remarks made about him. Beyond that, not even luck can make certainty possible. The rest is merely printed matter, and a harassed man who sweats out his life in libraries, courthouses, record offices, vaults, newspaper morgues, and family attics. A harassed man who knows that he cannot find everything and is willing to believe that, forever concealed from him, exists something which, if found, would prove that what he takes to be facts are only appearances."*

Bernard DeVoto " The Skeptical Biographer" used at the beginning of Wallace Stegner's *The Uneasy Chair*

June 2022

## Sunflower Summers

They are everywhere this year—right now. The lovely scraggly sunflowers of my Kansas youth. Not the sturdy nine-footers that gardeners covet for borders or birdseed. The ones with giant faces—often planted next to the hollyhocks. No, at the moment Montana roadsides and gravel pits and construction sites sport spindly plants a couple-three feet tall with small but exuberant blooms.

I think of them as Kansas—not Montana—flowers. We were, after all, the Sunflower State. And that symbol adorned all our tourist trinkets and maps and road signs. I noticed them as a child—and wanted so much to make bouquets of them. Bring them into the house. Savor that exuberant sunniness. And I didn't believe Mother when she said they were sticky and prickly and unlikely to survive. Until a trip to Coronado Heights* gave me an easy opportunity to pick a few. Mother, of course, was right and I couldn't get rid of the tacky adhesive on my hands until we got home to soap and water.

Sunflowers still make me happy. So when I began noticing their abundance around Helena I found more places to drive when I was out

on errands. Just for fun. Just to see sunflowers. And finally—years after my affection for sunflowers began—I realized that I didn't know why they were such cheerful roadside decorations.

Turns out there are easy answers. Those Jack-in-the-Beanstalk sunflowers are annuals—the species and seed long since honed to produce more seeds for human use. In contrast, the roadside plants are sometimes perennials, but for sure a species that re-seeds itself year after year. And here's the key: those seeds thrive in disturbed soil. The very sandy cut-and-fill stuff lining highways. Or mucked up construction and gravel excavations. Paved roads and trails provide even more of what sunflowers crave: the run-off from rainstorms, heat stored in concrete or asphalt, and unobstructed sunlight with few other plants tall enough to compete for air and light.

So our rather idyllic Montana summer—with just the right elixirs of sun and rain—and our housing construction boom have made those ordinary, sturdy sunflowers so happy. As they now do me!

*Coronado Heights is the southern-most bluff in a series of seven, known as the Smoky Hills. The hill is located northwest of Lindsborg, almost 30 miles from my hometown, McPherson. Supposedly, Francisco Vasquez de Coronado and his men viewed the prairie from this lookout point 300 feet above the valley floor. Chain mail from Spanish armor has been found in the area. In the 1930s, Works Progress Administration (WPA) men built the little stone castle atop the hill at Coronado Heights Park and stone picnic tables and fire pits nearby. It was a special spot for our family to picnic and classmate Curtis Rafelson held his birthday parties here every year.

**September 2023**

## Tiger Lilies

Our flowers loved this Montana summer: daffodils and tulips early on; iris and lilacs; and then when the days heated up delphiniums and petunias and zinnias and marigolds and morning glories and tiger lilies. A happy abundance we seldom see.

And so, driving around Helena, admiring gardens, I was returned to Gettysburg and the summer of 1973. I lived in the sweet garret apartment next to the National Cemetery—all dormers and gables. No furniture that counted except a bed and tippy ice cream parlor table. But a glorious life rich with work I loved at the Park; a bevy of friends; a sense of mastery and creativity. Able to entertain on those flimsy wire chairs, flirt, travel a bit, begin acquiring the stuff of a real household.

And one summer evening, I came home to an enormous bunch of tiger lilies left on the stairs to my apartment. No card. Just this bouquet tied into an armful of electric green and orange. Exotic, stunning—up close almost orchids with their velvet petals.

Tentative and discreet inquiries as to their origin came up empty. How could I not be curious then—and now? And touched. Rendered wistful. Except for the gardenia corsage that Steve Kubin's mother ordered for my prom date with Steve, I'd never been wooed with flowers. Well, and actually Mrs. Kubin's purchase didn't count either!

And may not have been then. But I've lived 50 years savoring the joy that a summer's evening gift of lilies gave me. Holding close the knowledge—not the possibility but the knowledge—that someone out there in my Park Service/Gettysburg universe cared. Cared enough to let those exuberant blooms—and the energy invested in gathering and delivering them—speak for themselves with no strings attached.

I run through the likely names and faces: Barb and Roger and their lively farm and art and garden; Glen and Marie—who offered motorcycle rides through the park at dusk; Audrey and Hank, my many-childrened neighbors in the Cemetery gatekeepers house; Betty and Joyce and Carmen and Mary and Nora, the local ladies who knew more than all the rest of us combined and kept the Park running; close friends Mike and Melinda; the summer rangers Alan and Jude and Bob—after all Alan had a crush on me; surely not Mr. Harrison or Newt or Jerry, the brass. The mystery endures. But picturing those colleagues and friends and the ties that bound us in those Gettysburg years remains as sweet as that armful of tiger lilies.

September 2023

## Connie – The Friend Who Believed in the Power of Sunsets

For the last three years, my day has ended with an email to Connie Waterman. Nothing long or complicated. A word or two about my day. A question about hers. Some weather observations. And always, always a valediction of love. I treasured her responses—crafted similarly—though periodically rich in details drawn from her memory. Her words and friendship brought my day to a peaceful close.

I learned to know Connie five or six years ago when my friends, Jackie and Peter Lenmark, invited me to join them in taking Sunday evening dinner out to Connie. "Out" because Connie lived in a historic farmhouse on the edge of Canyon Ferry Lake, about 20 miles east of Helena, at the foot of the Big Belts.

The Lenmarks had known Connie and her husband Norm for years—the friendship borne of shared community engagement, the legal world, Montana adventures. After Norm died a decade ago, the friendship deepened with those Sunday evening dinners and Peter's skilled attention to Connie's lawn and water system.

There were many Connies whom I didn't know. Or knew about only in the skinniest outline: young girl in a New York orphanage; college student; teacher; social worker who moved to Colorado; single fearless young woman; mom; wife; juvenile probation officer.

I knew the Connie who was the sum of those histories and adventures. Who rebelled against being in her 80s and the related debilities. The Connie who also wouldn't give up. Who—as through her life—saw and loved life's ridiculous moments, had the kindest heart, and still didn't suffer fools or manipulators gladly.

I knew the Connie who played mean hands of bridge. Who spent serious money on a stray cat. The Connie who loved all birds. Who nurtured especially her neighborhood flock of hummingbirds. Who could get down and weed her extensive flower garden. Who dressed stylishly. Who treasured a quick draw or two on a cigarette several times a day—apologetically and resolutely. And came to share an attentive, thoughtful daily-practiced friendship with me.

With just the slightest prompting, Connie loved to regale us with the hijinks that she and Norm got up to. She laughed at her own foibles: an absence of any sense of direction; her attempts to drive a stick shift and gas up her vehicle at the county pumps. She described characters whose eccentricities amused or bugged her.

But she was in deadly earnest when she talked about her philosophy of granting young people—including her probationers—her respect and encouragement. She had no patience for administrators who relied on punishment more than fair play. She reveled in telling us about her refusal to put her tall, beefy teenage charges in handcuffs as police had—despite her own diminutive stature. And she had no qualms about letting her juvenile charges provide directions to their homes. More than once, in those evening emails—as she considered her own life—she'd tell me that she thought—she hoped—that she'd made a difference in the world.

That first Covid year was difficult. Our Sunday evening dinners didn't seem safe. We tried Zoom. Connie played some bridge online. We

managed some gatherings outdoors on my porch or hers. Peter did yeoman's duty in working on her yard and house. That's when we began our evening emails. And a steady diet of jigsaw puzzles. But Connie was still more isolated than she'd been.

Early in 2021, after her dishwasher broke and damaged her kitchen floor, Connie asked Peter to take her to Bozeman to visit her daughter and son-in-law for the weekend. Cathy and Andy Grace are both physicians. They welcomed her to their extraordinary home at the edge of the Gallatin Valley, but quickly realized that Connie wasn't just tired. She couldn't get enough air.

Following a hospital stay, Connie returned to her daughter's house, on a steady flow of oxygen and hospice care. Connie died this past week—almost two years later—still writing those evening emails within a couple weeks of her death.

Early on in her stay at Cathy and Andy's, Connie remarked how strange it was to receive no real mail addressed just to her. Cathy had taken over bill paying and other business correspondence. I know the joy of real mail. So Connie's comment galvanized me to begin a mail campaign. Sending ready-made cards at first. And then evolving to ones that I made for her—poaching pictures from second-hand art and history, photography and natural resource books for one side and writing notes or adding quotations on the other.

I loved this small dab of creating and the imperative to get out of the house to the post office. The correspondence deepened our friendship.

Connie would comment on artists that she loved; historic photos prompted memories of her house parents and routines at the orphanage. She remembered what I wrote about my grandkids and mentioned that in her emails. I found a book of classic paintings in which the faces of famous people had been replaced with cat photos. Those were Connie's favorite cards!

For several years, we exchanged very proper, small Christmas presents. But the holiday before Connie headed to Bozeman, she called one afternoon while I was running errands. She was waiting, she said, in front of my condo and would continue to do so if I'd be home soon. I hurried but still kept her waiting before we could meet on the porch for her to hand me a big wrapped Christmas present. She didn't ask me to unwrap it then—but hoped I'd do so soon. I know that I waited longer than she wanted. In a burst of wonderful whimsy, she gave me a cat toy, a "Fling A MA String." She was so eager to see if my resident cat, Simon, would love it. Truth be told, he ignored it. But with enough small treats, I could lure him to its proximity and send Connie the photo. My new kittens, however, need no extra encouragement.

Cathy and Andrew's living room faced south and west—floor to ceiling glass delivered every sunset into their home. And Connie always always savored the beauty of those. She'd often describe the colors in them to me in her evening emails. And wished that I could see them—knowing that my predominant view is to east. She'd remark on her extraordinary luck to be where her day ended with such beauty. From September 10:

*Hi Marcella,*

*As always, it was a splendid sunset with the sun going down as a fiery red ball and the western horizon in all shades of pink and mauve. Every sunset I revel in how lucky I am to be surrounded by such a magnificent panorama of pink, purple, and mauve in all shades.*

*Love, Connie*

And on the evening of October 8—less than a month before her death—Connie sent this email. For me, Connie lives in these words of celebration and in "her" incredible sunsets.

*Hi Marcella,*

*Hope all is well with you and your kitties. I have just watched a beautiful evening sunset—fiery reds to all shades of pink, mauve and purple. I like to believe, perhaps naively, that if everyone could experience the quiet beauty of such sunsets, the world would experience less animosity and stress.*

*Take care and sleep well.*

*Love, Connie*

November 2022

## Heat

I adore these sun-scorched days. Days I begin by tucking up the house to capture the night's cool. And end when I open the windows, crank up the fans, and revel in the downward slide of degrees as dark comes on. I will always take suffocating heat to deep cold. And always sun and sky to vistas of snow. Even knowing that lightning and irresponsible humans will make fire from my favorite ingredients.

But this summer's heat has conjured memories. These ninety degree days have become a warm butter knife, slicing across time and space to other summer moments, to other places and people I've treasured. I remember . . .

Hot hot summer nights on Marlin Street when Mother and Daddy drove us around McPherson—inviting cool air through the wing windows. And stopped at the Rock Island train station so that Sonja and I could walk the rails until we felt vibrations under our sandaled feet. And then debated—in Pig Latin—whether to go for frosty A & W root beers.

Stifling Sunday afternoons when Daddy took us to his downtown insurance office and fretted over work while Sonja and I raced armless office chairs along the darkened cool aisles of desks.

I remember Mother's impromptu picnics. Hot dogs and green beans and potato salad. Laundry mornings launched early—the sheets on the line dry before we'd hung the rest of the wash. Or the house quiet because Mother was outside weeding ahead of the sun. The brisk chill of enamel pans on my bare legs as I pitted Grandma Sherfy's cherries or shelled Mother's garden peas. The steamy hell of peach canning days in our tiny kitchen, blanching each batch of fruit in boiling water. Kool-aid our afternoon treat.

Vacations to Indiana and Iowa that began at four in the morning to put bearable miles behind us. Then sips of cold, metallic water from the Little Brown Jug thermos when we turned heat-numbed in the black Chevy. Daddy forever afraid of that old Chevy overheating.

Long, late June wheat harvest days at the Dreshers. Daddy in his element helping Don and the boys. While the rest of us—females— orchestrated enormous tailgate lunches.

I remember. . . Gettysburg's stifling humid mornings in Mrs. Keefer's sunporch standing in front of a fan to don my green gabardine suit, girdle, nylons, and small brown heels. Summer seasonal garb. We vied for shifts in the air-conditioned visitor center and the darkened Cyclorama aerie. I was spared sun-baked Little Round Top—not safe for a girl in 1968.

I took that fan to Williamsburg for a six-weeks seminar in historic preservation one summer and understood immediately why the first Jamestown residents might not have survived the claustrophobic, mosquito-friendly sauna of a landscape.

Then this heat drops me onto Helena's Choteau Street and I'm doing dishes—sweating under the kitchen window as just a whisper of breeze and summer band concert music reaches me. Or, I'm hunched down among the raspberry stalks in the still, prickly heat—choosing distance from the girls' squabbling to basement cool. I picture the freezer stocked with water bottles—relief intended for our tribe of miserably hot rabbits in the garage or on show at the even hotter fairgrounds.

I remember my Carnegie library stints in the cooler half-basement children's department. And on the hottest days, Mrs. Eastham's generous gift of limeades from Raleigh's Drugstore even if—as the youngest employee—I was sent to fetch them.

There was that last semester of college when I sweltered over a book of softball rules in my dorm room. Written tests being my only chance for a decent grade in the required and hated sports classes. Really, the runners can't steal bases??

Still I also remember sweet sweet summer evenings at Kendrick Legion field with Dave and the girls watching our rookie league pro baseball teams—dodging setting sunshine in the old, splintery wooden bleachers—still cooler than the fresh-faced boys from Arizona and Puerto Rico all with dreams of the majors.

Then that butter knife of memory slices into another time and place. Fourth of July fireworks across the Potomac as Bob and I cuddled on our blankets in Arlington Cemetery. Or treated ourselves to elegant picnics on summer afternoons at Wolf Trap—Gilbert and Sullivan or Rodgers and Hammerstein the backdrop.

I summon our North Fork days when the girls kept vigil by the porch thermometer—waiting for the mercury to reach 80—the temperature that Dave required to float the river. I remember even more poignantly those sun-kissed, damp, tired girls asleep in the back of the 4-Runner as we drove home to the cabins to photograph fish and fall into bed.

I am remembering the years when no power on earth—more specifically no heat—would have kept me from the pastures outside of White Sulphur Springs for the Red Ants Pants Music Festival. And the chance to dance under the stage to Ian Tyson and Corb Lund and

Rodney Crowell and Red Molly and Parsonsfield.

And, in turn, those memories lead me to the July when I met Jean and Bryan on the train in Shelby for a Montana expedition—replete with broiling rodeos and powwows and boat rides and too much wine sitting outside an aging East Glacier motel—just in time to watch the saddle horses coming home from their day of tourist transportation.

Preceded by the life-changing magic and daunting humidity of Patmos—that brought music and precious new friendships and a commitment to words—these among others.

Finally that slicing knife of time comes back to this week in 2006 and a night so hot that Dave—still recovering from his stroke—chose to sleep in our basement while I went upstairs. Only to find him gasping—stretched across our bed in the wee hours. And then to hold his hand two nights later—as a radiant July sunset lit his dying face.

In the days following all I could do was move the sprinkler around our lawn—and come back inside to fall into sweaty sleep—hoping desperately to wake to a different reality.

I am barefoot tonight. Planning evenings of root beer floats with friends—preferably on the porch—though not possible until the sun goes down. Or I'll make slightly sweet tea in a stainless steel bowl the way that the Gettysburg ladies taught me. I consider ice makers one of the great 20th century inventions. The cats—the boys—are ok but lethargic, still sleeping in spots that offer the illusion of cool. They came to live with me exactly two years ago. Before the smoke settled in, we had a month of startlingly beautiful, summer mountain and cloud drama. I will soon have a bountiful crop of tiny tomatoes for my friend Martha. With basil to match. I know better than to wear shorts. But if you catch me alone at home, I might be in a dress. The house hums with my current bevy of fans. I sleep well in their lullaby and those blissful night breezes.

I love this heat. And the summer memories that grow fast and hardy and poignant in these luscious, scorched days.

**July 2024**

# SEASONINGS

*"Life should be a little nuts.*

*Otherwise it's just a bunch of Thursdays strung together."*

*Kevin Costner spoke that little gem to co-star Jennifer Aniston in the not-very-famous movie Rumor Has It. The words are screenwriter Ted Griffin's. I paused the movie long enough to copy it for the refrigerator. And have since discovered that others heard the wisdom it offers.*

*I live a predictable, sweetly quiet life. A long string of Thursdays. (Which is, of course, the perfect weekday to use.) The years of rising at five a.m. to finish a project, catch an early flight, grab a state car, abandon the bathroom before Dave and Amanda needed hot water, assemble a company casserole, run to the subway are all well behind me. I've not baited any mining or power company executives for a long time. I'm on no corporate or public service ladder.*

*Instead, I sleep late, play internet Scrabble over that first cup of coffee, and then consider a shower. I might even scan several news feeds instead or read another chapter on my Kindle first.*

*Which means that I treasure the "seasonings" of my life all the more. The moments when stuff goes a little nuts, a little haywire. The unanticipated opportunities and frustrations, the spur-of-the-moment cocktail hours and grandkid visits, startling sunsets, the silly magpies scamming popcorn off the porch. A call that returns me to college. Times when I'm scared or excited. When I see something that intrigues or horrifies me enough to write. When I travel—always.*

*Some of those moments that season my quiet life follow—beginning, of course, with cats.*

## A Meditation on Cats, Rabbits—and a Pig

Let's start with the pig. She's Esther and she lives in Campbellville, Ontario, with her turkey brother Cornelius, her dog brother Phil, her cat sister Delores, and her dads, Steve and Derek. Given to her dads as a micro pig, Esther now weighs almost 600 pounds. She lives indoors, is housebroken, and can take herself outside as needed. She has, however, mangled most of Steve and Derek's major appliances at one time or another. And in various fits of pique, she's ravaged so many

mattresses that her dads now supply her with pink tumbling mats. Esther, of course, has her own Facebook page and a farmed-animal sanctuary created in her honor. To the delight of some friends and the disbelief of others, she has my full attention... and heart.

Less as a curiosity and more as a friend and morality tale. Esther doesn't talk, as such, but her dad Steve, who's devoted the last decade to her well-being, provides her voice. She is California girl funny, selfish, and phenomenally smart and clever. She doesn't need her dad to be smart and clever. That's all her. I try to see what she's up to every day. In these political, climate, and Covid times, Esther is the antidote to so much despair.

Esther and her dads are vegans. Without banging the drum of supercilious righteousness, they demonstrate why we all might want to rethink our dependence on industrial farming. Esther is the one (out of 700 million pigs around the world) who gets to wriggle with joy at a tummy rub and can fall asleep cuddled up with her brothers and sisters.

I cannot call myself a vegan or even a consistent vegetarian. I try. But not half as consistently as I could. I weigh my options frequently. For sure, though, Esther much influences my cat parenting and my memories of hosting a garage full of rabbits.

I adopted my first cat in 1973—a teenage Russian blue who came from Roger and Barb's Pennsylvania farm. Lord, he was a character. There was the day I came home to my historic garret apartment and found that he'd dug the dirt out of every single houseplant I owned. Sooty accompanied me on my inspection tour and then, before my disbelieving eyes, hopped into the bathtub and pooped. I can only wonder what he REALLY wanted to say. He's the cat that wouldn't abandon my Washington D.C. bed when Bob was there. He came to Montana with me, sedated in a cat carrier at my feet on the airplane and lived

until 1989. Sooty was the first of my cats that Dave tolerated...

Cat-rina and Shadow followed—felines that started life in Emily and Amanda's Columbia Falls home. Shadow had been Fluffy—but acquired his new moniker when he took to settling himself directly behind our heels—the better to trip us. Both cats crossed the Rainbow Bridge the year before Dave died. And with Dave's grudging but sweet OK, I brought Mr. Noodle home from the Humane Society the following March. A two-year-old, he'd been called Vincent, and Dave thought a name change in order.

Originally barred from our bedroom, Mr. Noodle joined me the night Dave died. And slept beside me most of the rest of his life. On Dave's side of the bed. He moved with me from our family home to this snug condo. After Mr. Noodle died, I wasted little time in adopting Simon. A ten-year-old, he'd been relinquished by a family increasingly allergic to cats.

Simon's a lean part-Siamese, though his conversation is ordinary cat, always with great eye contact. He is shy and scared, achingly so. The moment the front door opens he runs for cover. He is not nearly as happy as I am that four young grandchildren now visit frequently.

Zoom calls, the vacuum, and the disposal terrorize him. He's affectionate in his own way, rarely sleeping on my lap, but walking to and fro across it if I'm reading. He doesn't spend the night with me, but usually settles close for a few minutes and stares at me. He loves tunneling between quilt layers and will do anything to get me to rub his tummy and back. In the morning, he keeps vigil to see if I might be waking up. And then won't go away unless I pull the covers completely over my head. I am sure that he knows I'm still there, but he and I both pretend I'm not. He's the first cat in my life who uses his paw as hand—reaching for what he wants or pushing me away.

I almost said "he's the first cat I owned." But with Esther's help, I've come to rethink my verbs. Caring for. Living with. Sharing the house with… all seem more appropriate descriptors.

And about the rabbits. I would find it so easy to say that we "raised" rabbits—starting with two 4-H mini-lops. And, for the next 20 years, housing somewhere between half-a-dozen and 28, depending on the presence of new babies. Mostly harlequins as part of Amanda and Dave's intense period of rabbit shows and competitions. But once again, I'm no longer sure that "raised" has the right connotation.

We eschewed the 4-H rabbit manual's section on how to kill and prepare rabbit stew. We were having none of that. Showing rabbits at the 4-H fair involved Emily and Amanda, dressed in white shirts and black ties, standing behind a rabbit they had trained to sit still. And in scorching July days, keeping frozen water bottles in their cages.

Dave and Amanda soon realized that civilian rabbit shows were a possibility—and put together the fact that few people in our neck of the country owned harlequins. Having a rare breed upped the odds considerably for winning at shows. Dave devised a rack to hold rabbit cages in the back of our 1986 4-Runner. We covered a good deal of the West accompanied by the smell of warm bunny pee. Amanda was always on the lookout for new "blood." And Dave was about as excited for the birth of Solo, a beautiful baby harlequin, as he was for his daughters' arrivals. He kept sneaking home at lunch to check the nest box.

When Dave died, I was still caring for one remaining bunny. And didn't even consider moving as long as she lived. My role in the bunny operation was, in fact, largely care and feeding. Raising a bit of parsley, washing carrots, scraping pee-soaked papers off the metal bottoms of the rabbit cages and adding new papers. That last part was usually an end-of-day task—hurrying between the house and the garage under star-studded skies. On Saturdays, checking in with the local news agent to pick up carloads of outdated newspapers. Scrubbing cages on sunny October days—with wire brushes and paint scrapers—so that the cages would weather the winter in somewhat clean fashion.

I found it much harder than Amanda and Dave to hold the bunnies—what with their very strong back legs. So I mostly knew the bunnies as garage companions as I fed and watered them and tidied up their cages. Dave left a radio playing for companionship. We provided a heater to keep the temperature reasonable and the water bottles thawed. I would rub noses with the bunnies when they hopped over to the edge of their cages, pet them with the cage door open. And there at midnight, cry if I needed to, talk out the day's slights or pain. The bunnies' offered quiet eyes, utter acceptance, solace.

The rabbits who live in the Happily Ever Esther Farm Sanctuary enjoy their own Bunny Town, an outdoor space built with deeply buried, native rock walls and netting over top. A place where they can explore, sniff, hop about, sleep in a patch of sun safely in the day, be with each other. At night or in bad weather, they are escorted into small adjoining houses with straw flooring. Sometimes they share space with rescue chickens.

Our bunny-raising practices mimicked those of the 4-H rabbit leader. We read books. We bent over backwards to address everyday bunny ills. Casually considered bringing the bunnies indoors but were deterred by cats who might be aggressive and electric cords that would be fatal if chewed. Even then, progressive books told us that bunnies could be litter trained. But...

In hindsight and with some flickers of understanding then, I could never be sure that we were good rabbit caretakers. A garage full of cages. Wire mesh always underfoot. Maybe music from KBLL that the bunnies detested. Long long hours when no one appeared. No opportunity to cuddle with a brother or sister. And only the rarest occasions to be outdoors on grass. Though when they were, their leaps and corkscrew whirls showed us nothing but joy!

Scientists of all stripes now explore the intellectual and emotional intelligence of animals. After millennia of asking no such questions, we've now started wondering just what our animal companions and those who appear on our plates might know and feel. So much of our culture depends on never asking. Esther, in all her enormous pink glory, has, for me, become the summons to drop the cover stories that humans have told since time immemorial: that animals experience little pain; that they are dumb; that, in the hierarchy of creation, they are less important; that we are "owed" their service, their companionship, their entertainment, their flesh. Drip by drip, the news brings us information to the contrary—one study, one creature at a time. Anthropomorphism may, turns out, be less a vice or a dodge and more a reality.

For me, that means that when Simon calls for attention, I will take the time to give him some. To shift the pattern from those days when we traveled so much, worked so much, played so much that Sooty and Cat-rina and Shadow were nice appendages to our lives, but rarely a priority. When the garage full of rabbits existed not because we sought their companionship and enjoyed caring for them, but for their conformation. We genuinely loved all our pets, but our interactions with them occurred—as **we** had time and energy more than when **they** needed it.

Simon remains inscrutable. But I try now to talk with him often. And when he dashes down the corridor and stretches out on his side, why wouldn't I scratch his belly. Retirement gives me the time. Esther gives me the inspiration to be at his beck and call rather than the reverse.

**February 2022**

## No Cloudy Days

My Simon, my white ghost, my sun-seeking companion left this world Monday afternoon. As always, my heart breaks more viscerally when my cats die—than even the humans who've lighted my way. In their last days, especially in their last moments, I am desperate to speak "cat" and to tell them of my love, thank them for theirs, ask forgiveness for all the times I didn't divine what they most needed. I know only to employ human words to share my heart. And tears and touch.

I can never really fathom how any nonhuman species accepts us, moves into our lives and trusts us with theirs. It is the stuff of miracles. And so so often, we abuse that trust with our conviction that we are owed the lives of other beings. That they exist for our comfort, our hunger, our curiosity, our experiments, our loneliness.

Simon spent the first decade of his life in another family's home. Relinquished ostensibly in the face of allergies. But already named. And so I began our time together wanting cat words so that Simon could tell me his routines, his preferences, his troubles. To know

what he was experiencing. From a home to a room full of cages and a series of humans sizing him up for possible adoption. Vulnerable, scared.

Whatever the look of quiet desperation in his eyes— there at the Humane Society—Simon made his fear and displeasure known ever so loudly the moment I put him in his carrier. As we crossed through the building and settled him in the car, the vet tech kept murmuring, "nothing wrong, just a cat going home" to keep other employees from rushing over. Simon yowled until I opened the carrier here—where he could run free.

At which point, he made a beeline for me. I'd collapsed on the sofa to take a breath. And for the next 30 minutes or so, Simon climbed across my lap again and again—hunting for a fist, an elbow, my nose, anything solid to head butt. Purring loudly. I took all that to mean that he appreciated his new home, that he felt safe.

But then, after a couple laps around the house, he unerringly found the back of the closet and a little footstool that my dad had made in high school shop class—and curled up beneath it. Short of regular litter box trips, the occasional midnight run, and eating, he never emerged for a couple months. I took his food and water to the closet.

Those odd midnight runs were reconnaissance missions. I'd find fur in unusual spots—newly clawed chairs. And ultimately, Simon's arrival on my bed. In fact, for a few nights, he'd burrow under the covers to sleep on top of me. Then, a couple nights later, next to me, above the blankets. During the day, he resumed his spot in the closet. Finally, I began moving his food and water out from the closet—a little at a time—toward the kitchen. And so he followed his nourishment into the rest of the house. Except when anyone came to visit: friends, family, the vet. Once he realized I was on to him, his next ingenious hidey hole was the inside of the recliner. Not a whisker showing.

The shyness, the fear persisted except for a few visiting voices. When company left, he'd run from wherever he was hiding to find me shutting the front door. But Simon's idiosyncrasies kept evolving. He always treasured water: fresh bowls of it. Ice cubes added. Any glass that I was drinking from. Dirty dishes soaking in the sink. Then the toilet. And in this last week, a full bowl of freshly run water in the bathroom sink. And he didn't have either kidney disease or diabetes.

He was not a traditional cuddler. As in that first afternoon, Simon showed his affection by walking to and fro across my lap. Gentle head butts. Discreetly staying in my vicinity. Joining me—every single time that just the two of us were here—in the bathroom. In the morning, once I was up, he'd dash from the bedroom to the living room and flop over on his side for belly and back rubs. In the evening, he'd reverse the process by hopping up on the bed for the same massages. And at night, most special of all, once the lights were out, he'd come for a while to stretch out along my leg, with my hand underneath his warm belly.

He hated the vacuum and even the iRobot. He was skeptical about Zoom and where those unknown folks were. He despised the volume being up too high on computer or TV programs. And I think he disliked most of the music I liked on YouTube: good country, Queen, Americana, Tchaikovsky.

Once the sun was up, Simon hoped—fervently—that I'd get up. A preference he indicated by sitting at the top of the pillow and stretching his claws out toward any available flesh. He was very inventive about finding open skin. But if I pulled the covers over my head completely—even though he knew I was still there—he'd hop off the bed to watch again for some signs of my emergence.

Simon used his paws as hands more than any other cat I've known. And he was ambidextrous. If I'd scratched between his ears too long, his paw would snake up to bat my fingers away. Those little pink and white feet seemed almost as effective as opposable thumbs.

However lousy Simon was feeling this last week, he remained a sun-seeking spirit. This was a good time of year for him, as patches of light angled across the carpet early—often just his size. Of so much that I hope for him as he moves into the universe, I wish him sunlit hours most of all and a memory of how much I loved him.

**June 2022**

## Kittens

Hard to know whether the outrageous sum I paid Lowe's for three pots of fake Boston ferns anchored in concrete was money well spent.

On the one hand, I managed to save the heirloom begonias that flourished in the antique fernery. Heirloom being ones that came originally from Dave's bachelor apartment 40 years ago. And the fernery from Mother.

On the other hand, the artificial ferns appeal to the kittens just as much. They are given to making running leaps up into the sea of plastic fronds. Wiggling their small butts and stretching out as if they were outside among branches. Camouflaged. Ready to pounce undetected.

The begonias wait on the porch to be transplanted into smaller pots. And I haven't a clue where I'll put them so that they will be happy and safe. The only other two "real" plants in the house are swathed in tin foil—a texture kittens are supposed to dislike.

I brought these boys home little more than a month ago. And changed their Humane Society names to the oh-so-unoriginal Tuxedo and Tiger Tiger. Tiger Tiger comes from William Blake's poem, "Tyger Tyger burning bright..." Tuxedo is wearing one. The sleekest, perkiest formal wear I've ever seen.

My heart broke when Simon needed to make his way to the next life. As it did when Mr. Noodle made the transition. But I can't live long without a cat. Almost perfect companions, I think.

This time I let all of a month elapse and then adopted two—as recommended by the Humane Society. A bonded pair, though not siblings. And in another switch for me—true kittens. As I write they are currently almost four months old.

They have progressed from living in a kitty play pen, to the bathroom, to my bedroom, and now—for significant blocks of time with many toys available—to the rest of the house. I won't tell you how many times I've been to the pet store in the last month or heard the clerk say, "ooh, spoiled cats." I've never raised human toddlers, but I'm operating on the premise that diversionary tactics are important for my sanity and either cats or children.

In fact, I am alternately enchanted and beside myself.

Tiger Tiger is a diminutive, intricately marked baby wild cat. Polite and deadly. Of the two, he's especially enamored with outdoor smells and action, sitting for long spells on a windowsill. A little more reserved. But also more independent of me and his buddy. Slower to eat—which has its consequences. I worry that his family removed him from his mother too soon. In the middle of the night, Tiger Tiger cuddles as closely as he can to my face and licks every available spot of skin—purring loudly. I am reduced to silly giggles when he reaches my ear.

Tuxedo is all legs and bounce, accentuated by those two white gloves, two white spats, his immaculate bib, and a shiny black coat. Rather like a child, he does not walk. He runs, hops, and leaps. And those leaps are getting longer and longer. My living room is two leaps wide. The larger and lankier of the two, Tuxedo is something of a debonair bully. A Great Gatsby kitty. He beats Tiger Tiger to most toys. Gobbles his food and begins to push his little nose into Tiger Tiger's dish. And views all treats as HIS. He's also more overtly affectionate. When I return after a spell of being away, he stretches up and puts his paws on my chest and his face next to mine.

Battery-operated toys catch the boys' fancy. They are mesmerized each time I turn one on—even if it's for the 15th time that day. They are also intoxicated with feathers. Cat manufacturers are right to make many versions of mice, birds, and fish. However many epochs of breeding as domestic cats have elapsed, the guys recognize prey that they might have enjoyed out in the wild. The two also love mirrors and their own reflected cuteness.

And really, these boys do not need commercial entertainment. They have each other—tails, ears, legs, tummies—always available for pouncing, biting, and strangling. Seemingly without damage. Tiger Tiger initiates the mayhem as much as Tuxedo. When the two came home from the required snipping, I found it virtually impossible to enforce the recommended bed rest—inactivity. I could hijack all their toys—but not each other. At the moment, they are puffed up like Halloween cats, tails bushy, dancing sideways towards each other, glaring. They'll meet each other in a mid-air leap. And in about ten minutes, collapse together on the bed.

I try to look at the house through their eyes. None of the labels that I use—wing chair, Talavera vase, cat tree, kitchen counter, desk, window screen—means an iota to them. I believe they are thinking: big jump; smells of cat food; feels good to scratch; bug just outside; where's that barking dog; too far to jump—except, I CAN go HERE and then THERE and then THERE and I'll be up high. Seen through kitten eyes, the whole house is a delightful jungle gym. How on earth would they know which objects are sacred and which expendable.

Cat aficionados discourage spraying water as a disciplinary measure. It might work, they concede, but your cat is likely to resent you for a long while. Current experts recommend rewards for good behavior. I'm trying a clicker system: getting down OUT of the plastic ferns—one click and one treat. What's astonishing (Pavlov wouldn't be surprised) is the effect of one click. Tiger Tiger and Tuxedo are at my feet and they know that I'm wrestling with the package to extract their little tasty nugget. I'm not the least bit certain that the cats link their corrected behavior—getting out of the phony ferns—to the sequence.

I am sad that so many cat owners do not invest in spaying and neutering—services which are often free. But I am tickled to work with extraordinarily professional and kind Humane Society staffers who go out of their way to care for all the kittens dropped on their doorstep.

In adopting Tiger Tiger and Tuxedo, I'm indulging myself. My longing for companions who will be here when I come home. To whom I can say "good morning," grouse about winter, and cuddle. As I did the day Simon died, I wish for true "cat" communication skills. To know whether these little guys feel safe and loved. I know that they are smarter, more intuitive, emotional than we assume.

In fact, I'm inclined to think that pets—if we let them—teach us much more than we reckon about the complexity and wonder of all life. About the sweetness and intelligence and caring that they possess—when the human world often does not.

August 2022

## Confluence: The Boys at One
### And Marcella at 76

Sometime well after I'd acquired Tuxedo and Tiger Tiger, I did the math. And realized that when they reach 15, I'll be 90. What was I thinking? I don't even **see** myself at that age.

Of course, I didn't know what I was getting into last July when the Lewis and Clark Humane Society held an adopt-a-palooza. Simon had died three weeks before. The house was unacceptably empty. I was intrigued by a Bozeman friend's acquisition of two kitties. The Humane Society promoted the advantages of adopting two or more together: company and entertainment for each other. And the unspoken reality—more homes for the hundreds of kittens who would arrive on their doorstep all summer.

So that day came with reduced adoption fees. Two kittens for the price of one. Lines out the door. Bouncing kids, cautious parents. Businesses sponsoring cats. Friends "buying" cats for friends. I didn't even get past the front room—lined with cages—and a ten-week-old pair of cutie pies.

The two I spoke for weren't siblings but had been cage buddies. Mouse and London Fog to the Humane Society staff. In a fit of banality, I christened them Tuxedo and Tiger Tiger. Tuxedo, of course, is wearing one. Four white spats, a white bib, and a long streak of white down his tummy. Tiger Tiger is a mackerel tabby—whose fur is an intricate blend of fish-bone patterning and tiger stripes, black, gray, and caramel. Why two Tigers? The William Blake poem:

*Tyger Tyger, burning bright,*
*In the forests of the night;*
*What immortal hand or eye,*
*Could frame thy fearful symmetry?*

I've taken to making up my own last two lines of the verse—doggerel, different each time. Tiger Tiger is not impressed.

Tuxedo is an imp, a scamp, a rapscallion who walks cowboy bow-legged. There is no surface in the house too high for him. He can take off from the middle of my bed and land six feet down the corridor. Going after a toy mouse or a moving snake, he doesn't just run and catch, he pounces. Once he is sure I've settled for the night, he comes to sleep in the crook of my knees. His fur is expensive black mink and his body oddly muscular. He is not at all willing to sit on my lap, but is a champion leg rubber. He'll follow me, meowing for attention. And then fling himself down in front of me—on his back, sharing his long streak of tummy white—asking for a belly rub. And if I say "up up," he'll hop onto the bed and repeat the trick so that I can rub his tummy without getting dizzy in the process. If I end our belly rubbing session too soon, Tuxedo will put his paws on my chest and stare at me intently.

Tuxedo's best trick of all—hard to believe every time it occurs: he fetches. In the right mood, he'll find one of his hybrid bird/mice (created by someone who captured the best attributes of both species) and bring it to me—lots of leg rubbing to get my attention. And when I throw it, he brings it back. Repeatedly. Recently, he's begun fetching those light-weight practice golf balls.

Tiger Tiger is soft—body soft and fur soft. Silky. And personality soft as well. He too is not a lap cat, but a snuzzler. He comes right up on my chest, tucks his head under my chin, and begins cuddling and

nuzzling—well, and licking and kneading. Snuzzling. We share kitty kisses—or Eskimo kitty kisses with a little nose rubbing. There are days when he comes for snuzzles three or four times. And days when he stays on the back of the sofa bird watching. He's the cat most impatient for treats and human food. For escaping to the garage. He's been slower to leap to high shelves. And when he was little, just plain cautious. I find it easy to worry about his well-being in the face of Tuxedo's bullying. But when the two buddies began play-fighting, Tiger Tiger is usually the aggressor.

I've spent a small fortune on toys for the boys. Many of them battery-operated or USB port energized. When the kitties were small, toys that wiggled or spun distracted them from dangerous or destructive behavior. Many devices missed the manufacturer's promises. And the kittens grew bored with some. Over the long haul, the most captivating toys have been the cheapest: long sticks with feathers and bells or those bice—those bird/mouse combinations. In fact, the boys love freebies: ribbon, a length of rope, dishwashing scrubbies, Q-tips, a swinging cord attached to window blinds, a fly outside the window, magpies getting suet, a flash of sun reflected by glass onto the wall.

This morning, I found the two of them engrossed in catching a baby spider running around under my glass bathroom scales. They succeeded in moving the scales and reaching their prey.

Of well-spent cat money, I count the floor-to-ceiling climbing post at the top of the list—though it required multiple rounds of reinforcement from Bryan and Peter. The next best purchase was a Litter Genie.

Tiger Tiger and Tuxedo remain closely bonded. Tiger Tiger figured out how to open all my lower cabinet doors—bathroom and kitchen. Tuxedo watched and became equally adept. If Tiger Tiger—from his perch on the back of the sofa—spots a juicy bird, Tuxedo will come running from other rooms. Let one knock a pan off the kitchen counter and both of them will scamper away—and then peek around a corner at me, sharing the guilt. They'll cuddle up together on my bed in the afternoon, grooming each other. Or both amble out to the living room and take up posts in my vicinity but not right next to each other.

I've never quite bought unconditional love in a human arena. Fierce love. Protective love. Joyful love. Love deep enough to see past a hundred flaws and insults. Unconditional seems a stretch. You may feel differently. But I'm besotted with the boys. Kittens or big boys now—they attach no human meaning to a big bouquet of silk flowers or the marble bookends or the begonia plant that dates to Dave's apartment on Hoback Street. The house is their jungle gym. How on earth could they distinguish between a whirligig commercial toy and the green peas I just dropped on the kitchen floor?

I have friends who recommend a shot of water—to help them learn "right from wrong." In another life, I might have succumbed. Instead, I now belong to the "praise good behavior" school of thought, the "let's distract them" methodology. And for sure, the "pick your battles" framework. I find it a wonderful blessing that my best friends tolerate the boys investigating dinner from the unfilled chair at the table.

Most of this past year's training was mine. That begonia plant is the only living one in the house. The ferns in the fernery and the cactus on my desk came from China. I try to remember to put the dishwashing scrubbies beyond the boys' reach. I have a lidded cup for the water I drink all day long—otherwise I'd be sharing.

Two cats, of course, amount to more than two. They are a more complex, funnier, more maddening and more intriguing blend. Dare I say, a bit of a family. Not rivals to the grandkids, but still now home to me.

So I am one more old lady who loves her cats. The boys infused this year of aging, this year of an endless, ugly winter with laughter and wonder and love. Amanda when she was little spent hours studying her kitty Cat-rina. Also a brown, black, and grey tabby. I do the same, now, with the boys. Even more comforted by their quirks and their beauty. Perhaps most of all, I am made whole by their attachment to me. The belly rubbing that they request. Tuxedo's pure joy when I throw him the mouse. Tiger Tiger's snuzzling when a warm, soft ten pounds of cat helps me forget my uncooperative knees.

If these two cats are that wonderful, I think about the rest of the creatures on this planet that I don't know as well. The intricate miracles of sunlight and thunderstorms and super moons and osmosis. The beings on this earth that I've not yet had the privilege to meet. And might never. Bless the boys who spark those wonderings, those awarenesses—antidotes to the limits and losses of aging.

Here's to cats! Here's to wonder!

July 2023

## Drawing the Line

I was in college, but likely on holiday. Mother and Daddy and I were driving home from somewhere—the Dreshers maybe. I considered myself grown up and wise but was still in the backseat of the 1964 Dodge Dart. I watched Mother loosen her coat and start fanning herself—while the car heater roared. So, with newfound cockiness, I said something like, "Mother, why don't you ask Daddy to turn down the heat rather than suffering silently." To which my dad said, "But I'm cold. Now what do we do."

Our family, our church took the admonition to "turn the other cheek" seriously. To the point of pacifism. To the far wall of loving our enemies. Of all the Church of the Brethren beliefs, our response to violence defined us most. My church ancestors were imprisoned for refusing to fight in the Revolutionary and Civil Wars and in World War I. During World War II, they were shamed but offered alternative service.

I understand the inherent rightness and goodness of seeking peaceful solutions to violence.

I've also come to believe that in global matters and daily life the precept can be deceptive, disorienting, destructive.

I'm not advocating war. I so wholeheartedly believe in employing diplomacy and sturdy resolve rather than fists or missiles—when at all possible. But I was born at the end of a war that witnessed the Nazis systematically kill 15 to 20 million people. There are always historical "what ifs" that might have changed the course of twentieth century events. But scholarly speculation now cannot save those 20 million.

Nor am I advocating personal cruelty or ridicule or small sabotage or ugliness among friends and colleagues. I believe passionately in kindness and understanding and good manners. For walking those miles in others' shoes and lives.

But—astonishing and silly and obvious as it may now be in this time of my life—I have come to realize that pacifism and a family penchant for avoiding conflict created deeper injustices, more insidious pain. Small martyrdoms, silent suffering, behaviors and words that ate at our souls. Maybe not fatally, but debilitating nonetheless. That in being unguardedly open to the arrows of others' discontent or anger or unreal expectations or demands, I missed out on joy and dignity—and energy. As did our family—and as did and do many good families.

This is so not a new concept. Thirty years, at least, of self-help books have preached the importance of setting personal boundaries, of keeping "toxic" people at bay, of self-care as a foundation for loving others. Albeit some of that talk is mildly nauseating and unbalanced in other ways.

But I've found that my passive upbringing sent down hellishly deep roots. In fact, at the moment I'm picturing an exuberant weed common in Helena's older neighborhoods. I know it only as "hell's bells." It produces a stalk of leaves with little purple flowers. It mimics its neighbors. In a tulip bed, it grows only eight or nine inches high. Next to the delphiniums, it surges up to match their lofty spikes. And worst of all, it sends down nests of white carrot-like roots that no amount of excavation or Round-Up kills. If anything, eradication efforts spawn a new crop of healthier plants.

I feel like the words and examples of my childhood match those evil weeds. By spells in my life, I've known and felt the moments where a small, clear "no" or, as we do with pets and toddlers, a hand raised as a stop sign, would have been warranted. Would have saved hours of second-guessing, of hurts savored rather than resolved, of unexplained distancing. I've remained silent. My head knows better. But the best my heart and tongue could muster were forms of doublespeak and silence.

In the months after Dave's death, I didn't have the emotional energy to pretend agreement or tolerate ill-advised remarks or behavior. I remember the clearness I experienced when I said—nicely I think—what I wanted and needed.

I know—pretty deep in my gut—that setting limits, drawing the line, when faced with something antithetical to my heart or integrity will be hard. Maybe among the toughest challenges of these years. That— if I succeed at all—I may well be written off as old-lady-crabby or newly deluded. I'm quite sure that I'll bungle and misjudge moments and choices. And I don't wish to erase or dilute the impulse toward joy in which I spend most days.

But I still crave learning to utter the occasional "no." The periodic but firm, "I don't agree." The rare but heartfelt, "Not now." Or as a friend suggested, finding modest, non-inflammatory words that still convey honest feelings: "Ouch" for instance.

Summoning and speaking that honesty might just be a winter's project. I can practice on the kittens.

And, those long years ago in the car with my parents? Of course I had no ready answer!

**November 2022**

## Small Grandson

You gotta love a seven-year-old grandson who can't get over the odd pattern in the tines of a salad fork that don't exist in the regular one.

Or asks that his next birthday present be an old-fashioned Bissell carpet sweeper—that to his eye works just fine without all the noise of a vacuum.

Or wonders why on earth I go to the trouble of putting six colorful throw pillows on my bed when I only need one for sleeping.

Really two, since he was inclined to join me here rather
than stare at the little red light
on the TV from the guest bed.

He's often a solemn small
guy, but delighted to free the
bounds of earth chasing scarves
out of a science museum air
machine. Or scrambling up a
climbing wall, happy to let go
and bounce down when the
next handhold is out of reach.

Practical, when I apologized for
our water bottles heating up in the sun, he said, simply, "It's water."

Instantly competitive when sharing the opportunity to pitch against
another kid at a machine that recorded the speed of his fastballs. Or
against himself on those climbing walls: "This time I'll see if I can go
all the way around on purple."

Modest. He made darn sure that I was busy and NOT inclined to
help when he took his shower.

Gullible. At precisely the age to take miracle cures and science experiments on YouTube as gospel. Of course you can put a banana on top
of a cactus and grow a banana. And he watches a lot of YouTube—
preferably when eating.

A budding cook, in complete command of his own perfectly fried
breakfast egg or of a hot dog-ramen combo.

Vocabulary rich, and even more important, willing to ask the meaning of a word or phrase that he didn't know.

Free, for a couple days from the gang of three sisters whom he per-
ceives to make his life a misery.

And caught, in all the contradictions of being a little boy trying to "man up" when, in fact, he'd rather be comforted.

I am still ruminating on his current motto, his strategy for dealing with those pesky sisters: "A punch for a pinch."

I counseled walking away. Taking the fun, the reward, out of such encounters for the pinch-er. He was stupefied—disbelieving that I'd advocate such an approach.

But isn't it really the billion dollar question around our globe: when do we punch back against pinchers or when do we walk away. And will they stop?

July 2022

## Connections

A couple Saturday nights ago, I gathered by Zoom with my sister, Sonja, and her two sons, Ben and Tim, and daughter-in-law Lori. Borne of the exigencies of Covid when a summer reunion proved unwise, this conversation was maybe our tenth such Saturday evening confab in the last two years.

Early on, Ben suggested that we identify a topic for each call—based on something we all read or heard. We've taken turns suggesting background material: a short story; online museum exhibits; Native origin stories; aging; housing needs. Our conversations dance through and around those topics and sometimes touch on the week's biggest stories. But not a lot. We try to wrestle faithfully with the theme for the evening.

Afterwards, I was struck by how much and how little our occasional Saturday conclaves resembled family letters from my past.

My dad's family, the Sherfys, loved words. His father attended the Church of the Brethren seminary and prepared sermons the rest of his life. My dad and his three siblings all went to college—teachers in the making. My mom was one of two siblings among her eight who also put herself through college and taught school for almost a decade. My growing up was word and idea rich, grammatically correct and language colorful.

And for as long as I can remember, my parents received a fat envelope stuffed with an assortment of letters—different stationery, handwritten, typed. The Circle Letter—a "chain" letter circulated among my dad, his three siblings, and his mother. The siblings themselves didn't always write; sometimes a spouse pinch hit. The deal was that when the Letter arrived you removed your old missive, read the remaining letters, and added a new note to the packet. In that era of frugality, you weighed the new bundle, added just the right postage, and sent it on to the next person on the list. There was a suggested deadline for writing and forwarding the whole parcel.

As grandchildren began attending college and striking out into the world, Aunt Ethel, my dad's older sister, expanded the Circle Letter. It included the original participants and added in the growing-up group of next generation adults. All the same procedures applied.

But, the Circle Letter soon acquired complications. Chief among those, of course, was general tardiness and discombobulation among the younger set. We thought we were too busy with school and new careers to take corresponding with others as seriously. We lost the whole bundle once in a while. And we all dreaded notes or calls from Aunt Ethel or, God forbid our own parents, on the hunt for the irresponsible culprit. (The culprit didn't always fess up.) When the Letter made its rounds, news was often significantly dated.

My memory's a little dim here, but I think as the original four siblings grew older, they created their own Square Letter—rather than pestering the rest of us to participate responsibly in the Circle version.

Our Saturday night Zoom calls don't have a name—a geometric identity. They span two generations and occur, once more, among folks for whom words and thoughts are the coin of the realm. The Sherfys and the Griffiths. Two PhDs, several Masters, a law degree, a nursing and divinity degree. The "youngsters" all children of parents who placed great stock in thinking and speaking well. So far, we've been able to hold our calls to fit everyone's schedules. We usually talk for an hour-and-a-half or two. And settle on the month that might work for the next call.

Like the Circle Letter, our Zoom calls keep us in touch. With the added benefit of hearing each other's voices and seeing how we look. The topical framework steers us away from cocktail hour conversations that linger on weather or Trump or Covid. Although we give in periodically to banality.

What we gain especially from our real-time visits is the interplay of ideas, debate, questions that need more consideration. We are learning a bit about how each of us thinks. Our passions. Our vulnerabilities. What pushes our buttons. Who voices their ideas quickly. Who hangs back a bit. Who thinks as a teacher might. Who is dazzlingly well-read. Who remembers what they've read!!

Oddly, we may find it harder to tell each other about important changes in our lives—maybe harder than putting that news in writing. We almost didn't learn that Lori had been hired for a great new job. We are still shy with each other. And likely a bit reluctant to be emotional. But then those written round-robin letters were themselves carefully staged. We kept up family standards and imageries—gussying up our lives a bit for each other. Mildly competitive. For sure avoiding tricky issues. I was not inclined, for instance, to describe the lovely Manhattans I enjoyed during Friday night cocktail hour. Or Christmas on the Blue Ridge Parkway with Bob when there was clearly no ring involved. Or, explaining what galvanized me to seek extra help during my first fear-filled year in grad school: set against the high bar already established by most Sherfy cousins.

On balance, though, I think we've edged closer to being real in our Zoom sessions than we would in writing. Our Saturday night gatherings bring us into each other's homes. A dish of ice cream and comfortable chairs ringed around one of our living rooms would be wonderful. But even so—for sure with more fellowship than transcontinental travel would allow—we've come to be comfortable with each other. And for me, to gain deep respect and flat-out joy in learning to know my family—most especially that next generation—better than I ever might have in writing.

June 2022

## Within Earshot...

June 1968. Newly signed on as a summer ranger at Gettysburg—11 guys and me, we appeared in our brand-new Hart Schaffner and Marx green gabardine uniforms. Veteran ranger and summer supervisor Nick and the savvy locals—Nora and Mary and Colonel Sheads—provided our training. Lots of history. Lots of charts and maps and lists. Lots of jokes. Lots of protocols. One of which has lingered forever in my consciousness:

*Never never indulge in ridiculing visitors even after they've left the Information Desk. The moment that newly-arrived tourists catch knowing smiles or overhear pointed gossip their visit to the Park will be tainted. If—as staff—we can mock one set of folks, we'll likely subject the next set to the same cynicism or criticism.*

Dennis and I even managed to keep it together when a joker of a visitor came up to the Desk and said: I am a descendant of Father Corby (the Irish Brigade's priest) and Jennie Wade (the only civilian killed in Gettysburg). We said, "Sure, here's where you'll find Father Corby's statue." The long, sloping sidewalk into the Cyclorama Building gave us ample opportunity to size up each family, each busload of visitors. To consider but keep our considerations private.

If my life depended on it now, I could not spiel out the order of military groupings: company, regiment, brigade, division, corps, army. Or officer rankings. But that little tidbit about public courtesy—at least public caution—stays with me. And forewarns and forearms me.

In the end, it isn't about who's in earshot. Embarrassing others or myself. It's seeing the humanity in everyone around us. It's believing that they are doing the best they can in their circumstances, with their dreams and fears.

It's a lesson that I've needed to learn repeatedly. Made all the more real and pointed as I grow older, slower, less certain, more awkward.

And I'm thinking now of the people I saw as I traveled to and from the UK this month—the hundreds on planes and in airports. Recalling the internal critiques I allowed myself. And then—when I smiled at a person I'd disparaged in my mind—I saw life and joy and anxiety and realness. And myself.

May 2023

## Want Ads

We used to call them that—the classifieds that filled the final pages of our local newspapers. And we really meant everything advertised for sale in small boxes, divided into categories that included jobs available, pets for adoption, garage sales, used cars, and teenagers willing to shovel snow or mow our lawn. Or apartments to rent and houses being sold by homeowners. Sometimes "personals"—people seeking companions. Items lost and items found.

Studied with a bit of care that newspaper section was a periscope into a community: relative prices, the job market, the housing market. For a long time, those newspaper "Want Ads" served as a town's only employment agency and marketplace. Desperate for a job or a studio to rent, you had to get your hands on a current newspaper, circle the relevant ads, and find a phone to start calling.

That was then. Along came the internet and farmers' markets and Zillow and employment agencies and Zip Recruiter—and dozens of digital methods of buying and selling and advertising. Most of which included photographs—here-to-for not really an option. Most are free.

And Facebook. For our community, a group Facebook site: Helena Classifieds. I now can't recall why I joined a while back. Goodness knows I don't need more furniture or "décor." I'm decorated to a fare-thee-well. The toys I've saved for grandchildren will soon be surplus. And my retirement wardrobe focuses on the virtually-impossible-to-find comfy shoes.

But sign on I did. And some of the entries that I see in this season—appearing fast and furiously—are to be expected: artificial trees past their prime; boxes of Christmas ornaments; snowmobiles; wildly expensive tricked-out-year-old trucks; holly and ivy china sets that have been lingering on unreachable high shelves. Bunk beds from families whose children are growing; antique chairs too frail for holiday meals; dated stereo and TV stands; leather sectionals that won't fit in the new apartment.

But many of the posts break my heart. Crafts for sure of marginal quality:  knitted gnomes and hand-lettered barn-wood plaques; cocoa bombs. And then used items:  My Little Pony sets; a box of Size 4T boys clothes; a hand-tooled fringed leather purse from the 70s; earrings with a bit of jade showing; an odd assortment of children's books—sold job lot; a pair of name-brand high heels; stuffed animals—singly and in collections; five pairs of women's polyester pants, size XL; a gold necklace; tool sets; new-in-box Sorels; bedding; fabric; a Transformer toy set; wedding shoes never "wore." $15 will buy you two brunette hair pieces. $25 will get you an Italian silver wedding cake serving set.

The ads are laced with a variety of wiggle-worded claims:  just needs polish; you'll want to wash; right-corner scratch barely visible; almost no wear; gently-used; smoke-free AND pet-friendly home. And my favorite:  has developed a patina over the years. The photos themselves offer the same mixed messages.

I know that some mid-winter sorting may prompt these ads. Kids do outgrow clothes and toys fast. Christmas may bring an onslaught of new outfits and playthings. And ever since Covid, thrift stores here have been inundated—often closing their "receiving" docks. This isn't the season for garage sales.

But given the items, their pricing, and their use, I picture desperation. Items cobbled together to maybe make a saleable grouping; sentimental objects —with a bit of monetary value—unearthed; thrift store finds that might play to a larger audience. Most likely, the efforts of moms and dads struggling to find enough cash to buy new Christmas presents for children. In fact, every now and then, a parent explains: "raising money for teenage presents, Toys for Tots doesn't provide much for older kids."

I picture—who knows how accurately—adults lying awake at night trolling through their possessions mentally—trying hard to suss out something that someone might buy. Even if the items will have to be replaced—like tools. Like Sorels—warm winter boots. Food or heat or gas or gifts needed more. These aren't ads posted by Helena's sizeable homeless population. Nor obviously by upper middle class adults cleaning during this busy season. More likely from people whose hourly wages just just barely make ends meet. But not in winter. And not at Christmas.

A few ads turn the question around. Beginning with "**ISO**," in search of. Someone to shovel snow. A dining table with chairs. A free couch. Anyone traveling to Missoula on Friday. A lost dog. Again, both ordinary and desperate.

We are all truly **ISO** freedom from hunger, from the cold, from the ridicule of people who equate poverty with laziness or inability. Using the old terminology, we all **want** security for our families and those we love. Again—and here's the fundamental, fundamental part: without strings. The strings that come with paperwork and embarrassment and prostrating ourselves to stingy bosses or charities. Even without the struggle to raid our lives of belongings. Or sell, if not our souls, things we prize.

I have never ever had to scrabble just to survive. Thinking about it alone twists my gut in anxiety. On my own behalf and for those I picture behind the Facebook posts. I am so fortunate—lucky—through almost no special endeavor of my own. Geography, parents, timing, access to education dropped the Golden Fleece of an extraordinary life in my lap.

And without even visits from the ghosts of Christmas past, present, or future, I'm remembering what Uncle Mike and Aunt Helen once did—my godparents in North Manchester, Indiana. Helen taught first grade; Mike ran the Standard Station on Main Street. They loved children but didn't have their own. Mike played Santa most years, delivering presents to families—stealthily as requested by parents who also supplied the goods. And then without any fanfare or community involvement or waiting for "want ads," "Santa" delivered gifts that Helen and Mike just quietly purchased for households that they knew could use some help. I remain **in search of, wanting** ways to make that anonymous generosity deeper, more automatic in my life. I don't think that it's too late.

**December 2022**

## Voir Dire

I spent the lion's share of my 76th birthday in Helena's Justice Court. No, I was not the scofflaw. I was on jury duty—for which I managed to be selected out of something like 30 possible candidates. Of the 15 of us escorted into the court room, six of us—all women over the age of 50—were chosen to hear the case. Presumably based on voir dire—that process in which attorneys can question potential jurors and discard or select a given number to serve.

Voir dire is French for "to speak the truth." And lawyers and the judge counseled us to do just that. Most of the questions were obvious: did we know the defendant or the attorneys; did we have friends among the other potential jurors; had we ever been arrested, and if so, for what; had we experienced overzealous law officers. And, could we find a defendant guilty if we disagreed with the law he or she had allegedly broken. The questioning attorney gave us an example: say the legislature passed a law outlawing green hats and the defendant had clearly been seen wearing a green hat, could we

convict him. The group chorused, "oh yes." But I was hesitating—and the attorney caught my indecision. And asked for my answer directly.

I'm usually pretty compliant. Only late in life have I developed the ability to give texting drivers or ones who turn into the wrong lane, the benefit of my middle finger. I generally believe the speed limit is there for a reason. I've NEVER even considered shoplifting. In most ways, Paul and Esther raised a goody-two-shoes.

But I really did pause. I didn't focus on green hats. I was thinking instead of the spate of election laws so clearly designed to intimidate and discourage groups of voters. I was thinking instead of the ever-increasing number of laws designed to constrain women and dictate their choices. I was thinking of laws passed during the pandemic substituting political beliefs for those of health professionals.

And no—I had to say to the attorney—I'm not sure that I could find a defendant guilty in the face of some laws. Which makes me wonder why I was chosen for the jury.

The longer I think about the question and the truth I tried to summon—albeit hesitantly because it wasn't the answer for which courtrooms are designed—I've had some come-to-Jesus moments.

My advancing age and my retirement shield me from the much harsher, more frightening realities faced by so many of my brothers and sisters. I am long beyond child-bearing years and the dilemmas that I might have experienced. I've enjoyed the ease of mail ballots for a long time. I know when I'll receive them and when to return them. I don't need to take off time to vote. If I had to go to a polling place, I have a car and I drive. Medicare and a diligent general practitioner ensure that I get easy access to good information and preventive health measures. I've no reason to believe the balderdash that swirled around during the worst of the Covid pandemic.

In other words, way too many of the knotty moral and legal issues of our day—now captured in too many horrifying laws—haven't been MINE to experience. They've been a flicker too theoretical in my small, protected world. In the world where aging and manageable affluence serve as blinders, as buffers.

Voir dire—being asked to consider and speak the truth—before a very funky case took me a small step beyond theory.

But not nearly far enough, I'm thinking now.

The prosecuting attorney asked one other potential juror to explain her reasoning to the same question. To which she said, "I could find the defendant guilty, but then I'd have to take the question of green hat illegality up with the next legislature." A better legal answer than mine. And one that pointed the way to action not just theory. She was one of our six person panel too.

So the question isn't just whether I can and will speak the truth, after I've raised my right arm and sworn to do so. But whether I will act on the truths I believe. Whether I own the courage of my convictions and translate them into what I CAN do.

**October 2022**

# One Slim Device Away From Hoarding

Books are miracles. Their gradual, persistent emergence in our world changed every other element of society, over and over again. Their long, successful slog toward affordability and maneuverability bends my mind. Books have always been priceless. Almost beyond our grasp.

So I celebrate readers of all stripes and ages and preferences and interests. I don't really care how you read, only that you are a reader. Which is why I'm always knocked a bit for a loop when someone tells me—with a small edge of superiority, a soupcon of sanctimoniousness—that they prefer real books. That in order to enjoy a novel they must hold a tome in their hand, feel its heft. I understand their preference. And gracefully grant them that.

It's the sanctimonious part that niggles at me. It's the suggestion that real readers, informed people, true believers only read three-dimensional books.

Maybe, instead, they would be more in touch with the writer and her ideas if they could hold a clay tablet, or a slab of wax, or a scroll—once they've managed the mechanics of unrolling. Perhaps they'd like to hire a troupe or a troop of monks to copy and decorate a book just like the one their neighbor has.

I'm talking glibly... but honestly.

Why the disdain for publications that now live in the clouds, that—short of Mr. Bezos' extortionate strategies—are available anytime to anyone with some form of a baby computer?

I bought a Kindle before I took my first trip to Europe. Both were incredible luxuries. One was scary. One was comforting. Reading has always been my blankie, the warm elixir of words I've used to soothe myself through tough times. Escape. I couldn't imagine finding myself alone in Italy without a large enough stack of paperbacks to see me through 15 nights. Nor could I imagine toting all those around. I planned to carry no more than 20 pounds of belongings.

So Kindle it was. 2011 and we were still using stand-alone cameras, but in the great parade of book formats, the e-reader had appeared.

I haven't looked back.

Yes, I love bookstores and libraries and the exquisite process of browsing—of being intrigued by titles; noting authors who've produced a series of volumes; of admiring the artistry of jacket covers left on new books; of sampling categories outside my usual taste.

Yes, I miss the quality of photographs that "real books" include. I miss the ability to flip back to place the action on a clearly printed map.

But my Kindle brings me the ideas, the plots, the turns of phrase, the gifts of language and imagination that make so many books heartening, strengthening, dazzling. Nothing about my small screen detracts from the quality of writing, the enormity of thoughts.

I've got macular degeneration—so I revel in the luxury of changing backgrounds and increasing font size. I have a friend for whom reading text silently is disorienting. She treasures audible books.

And, without a Kindle in hand, my bedside stack of conventional books—unread or partially read—would tower to the ceiling. Now, when I settle into bed at night, I have, at my fingertips, almost endless choices for that evening.

And yes, if I substituted "real" volumes for the hundreds on my Kindle, you'd call me a hoarder. To find me, you'd have to weave through labyrinthine paths of teetering novels and essays and histories and biographies and scientific journals and poems. The dining table would be covered. The refrigerator bulging. Windows overgrown with climbing vines of words. The cat might have met an unfortunate topple. And I might have been smushed by the weight of all those pages. *

* *This isn't altogether fictitious. For a long time in my single life, I couldn't afford bookshelves. So I stacked my beloved tomes in tall piles, set a few on every step of a*

*stairway. Decorated with books. Organized books as the base of a table lamp. And paid a king's ransom in moving costs just to keep them with me.*

July 2022

## Who's In Blue

*"It is not the critic who counts; not the man who points out how the strong man stumbles, or where the doer of deeds could have done them better. The credit belongs to the man who is actually in the arena, whose face is marred by dust and sweat and blood... who at the best knows in the end the triumph of high achievement, and who at the worst, if he fails, at least fails while daring greatly, so that his place shall never be with those cold and timid souls who neither know victory nor defeat." (Theodore Roosevelt)*

God knows Dave didn't marry me for my sports acumen.

In a church college which had the audacity to interweave basketball grades with academic performance, I claimed a magna cum laude only by memorizing rules. When you can't heave a softball 60 feet between bases, your memory of whether runners can stray beyond the base line had better be perfect.

Or else you should be able to improve outlandishly in the space of a semester. Like my bowling score that skyrocketed from 10 to 92.

Given his attachment to sports, my 1982 courtship with Dave might have ended quickly had he not given me a new television on my October birthday. The 12-inch black and white model I'd purchased a decade earlier rendered World Series players fat, thin, and then AWOL as the picture rolled them into oblivion. Dave was having none of it.

Dave purely loved watching sports. He'd played most of them, even doing a stint with a minor league pro football team for college money. His dad had coached—officially and unofficially. The Walters held coveted and pricey Green Bay Packer tickets. The family joke/cautionary tale was this: It was New Years, also Dave's birthday, and the family had gathered to watch football. Dave's younger brother, Peter, brought a new girlfriend over. Who interrupted halftime festivities by asking "Who's in blue?" She did not make a second appearance.

Dave loved sports so much that we upgraded often—buying the latest and largest TV that we could. And as soon as we could afford it, ordered Direct TV sports packages. Spending leisure time with Dave in our Choteau Street home meant gathering in the basement rumpus room and watching whatever was in season. We'd be in our respective recliners, tucked up in old comforters. Sometimes squeezing work into commercial breaks. But often, just watching. I went to some pains to know who was in blue.

As Amanda came to live with us and launch her basketball career, we attended every home game and an astonishing number of road matches—middle school through college. Dave turned our backyard patio into a free throw circle—using traffic yellow—so toxic that he had to paint in stages.

Summer evenings found us at the Brewers rookie league baseball games in Kendrick Legion Field. Dave bought a program and scored each game. In March, if Carroll College hosted Class C basketball regionals—the small high schools scattered across western Montana—we took vacation to attend. Then there were Carroll's own games and Amanda's shot put competitions. I got proficient at assembling food for her track friends: yard-long sub sandwiches divvied up; Gatorade; cookies and peanut butter crackers. In other words, sports were almost as central to our lives as history and The Land.

My understanding of rules and patterns and fouls and plays varied sport to sport. I was pretty hopeless with hockey and football, though I much admired the skilled fearlessness of warriors on ice. Women's basketball was enough more deliberate than men's that I could follow it unfolding. Soccer hadn't caught on here yet. Track didn't count. I never tired of baseball.

My son-in-law now coaches small town Montana girls' basketball. And were Dave living, he'd be beside himself at the availability of a high school online sports network. Most Montana schools participate.

I'm that excited, too, in these wintry Covid times. And I'm tickled to realize that the lessons learned during basement basketball with Dave remain. Twice a week, these dark January days, I'm sitting here at my desk shouting, "She traveled!" or "NO, Simms touched it last!" or "For the love of god, you can make that bunny."

*Sadie Grove, Choteau High School, 2022, Choteau Acantha photo*

But now as always, I never tire of considering what it takes for a 17-year-old ranch girl or 18-year-old rookie from Guatemala, or for that matter, a seasoned relief pitcher to stand there alone. With the eyes of the world or the eyes of their parents and friends on them. When the outcome of a game depends on the pitch, the swing, the basket, the punt they need to make at that moment.

The rest of us face important moments, decisions that will have consequences, tests of our judgment or skill. But most of those occasions don't occur in an unforgiving public eye. Or in an instant that can never be recalled. In our world of words, most actions can be walked back, at least a bit—with a correcting phone call, an apology. We have time to think, to plan, to hedge our bets, to film a retake, to scrap one draft for another. Even musicians and actors can repeat a performance the next night.

Team sports allow players to lose themselves in group action, to be part of a moving screen or full court pressure or a strong-side run, a draw. Players become elements of a larger whole. They can anticipate and execute the next steps in concert with their teammates. But I watch for the moments when players stand alone—where the outcome of so much rests on them. When they either make a basket or don't. When they throw the perfect unhittable ball masquerading as a strike. When they field the crazy blooper that's found open turf and could have gone on bobbling forever.

The world does not turn on the outcome of a game or a race. Even though we sometimes act as if it does. But those singular moments of visible personal responsibility, of skill and focus required as the gym quiets, as a pitcher stares down the catcher—never lose their power for me. I hold my breath for those players. I imagine the magnitude of the responsibility they must be feeling, the wicked blend of fear and anticipation, the mental gymnastics at work, the slip of consciousness into motion. I am in awe.

Roosevelt's "man in the arena" speech has been beaten to death, often for causes that make me uneasy. And yet, hearing it brings me up short. I've never been in the arena. Or on the free throw line or in the batter's box. I have lived a life that did not create those do-or-die instances of terror and exhilaration. My come-to-Jesus moments have had parachutes. And I'm sedentary. Am I overthinking the all-or-nothing moments of sport? Does it all happen in a blur? I should ask. But in a universe where human behavior and skill still amaze and enliven me, I relish these freeze-framed moments of courage.

**January 2022**

## Shake It Off:  A Postscript to "Who's in Blue"

My son-in-law's girls' basketball team played their last game of the season several days ago. Most of the girls are young; some almost new to basketball. None were tall or solid enough to deflect opponents who were both. Nor were the girls able to power up shots from under the basket with any consistency. But they worked hard. And were not intimidated by their opponents. Or discouraged by widening gaps in the score.

And that persistence reminded me of another quality, another behavior I love to watch in play during games: refusing to linger in missteps, shaking it off, letting it go. The "it" in question is any kind of blunder: missing a basket, traveling, overthrowing a pass, stepping out of bounds. Any of the dozen moments in basketball's fast-paced action where a player makes a mistake.

In the office worlds I knew, the unease, the consequences, the "what ifs" of a mistake lingered. And consumed more head space than they warranted. I could drive 100 miles home from Missoula and keep returning in my mind to the moment when I should have said "hell no" to a slick contractor trying to ignore a historic site's significance. Or kick myself for failing to remember an argument that had worked with another agency. Even to fret over a meeting that became contentious rather than productive. Montana, you see, gave me many traveling miles in which to second-guess myself. Or to chafe over embarrassing moments. In fact, I was good at second-guessing myself even during a meeting. Symbolically taking my eye off the ball of the discussion in process and worrying over what I might have said.

I have an all-too-vivid memory of the price I once paid for wallowing in a bad experience. I'd had a sit-down with Montana University system staff, most especially their attorney. Universities—universally—functioned as little fiefdoms answering to no one and no law. And that behavior cost Montana a variety of historic buildings, gutted or torn down to satisfy a university president's ego. Notwithstanding the Montana Antiquities Act. The system attorney should have known better, but chose not to. After what I hoped would be a brilliant showdown and wasn't, I headed from the meeting in downtown Helena the two miles back to the Historical Society. At about 50 miles-an-hour in a 25-mile zone. And was pulled over for speeding and an expired driver's license. Before the afternoon was finished, I'd had to summon Dave for a ride to the courthouse, secure my new license, speak with traffic judge Myron Pitch, pay a fine, and call Dave for another ride to my abandoned car. Many lessons that day.

The Lady Bulldogs did none of that. Such behavior on a basketball court would spell disaster. The moment a basket doesn't fall, a player better commit to a rebound or a steal or heading up court with greater savvy and speed than the opponent. ANY mental time devoted to "oh shit, I should have made that basket" becomes a costly distraction. Compounds the risks. And morphs into debilitating self-criticism that undermines the automatic confidence needed for the next shot.

I suspect every sports fan knows this truism and takes it for granted. I suspect Matt taught that very behavior. Not all coaches—or parents—do. The line between coaching better skills and brewing self-doubt is a fine one. Because I hadn't been watching for a while, I saw the principle, the skill, with new eyes. And respect.

Watching Matt's team play, I could feel in my gut the angst that the girls MIGHT have experienced in those missed-shot, bad-pass moments. And I loved that they were all business instead. That they had already learned to shake off any of the frustration that I entertained and let it go. These players will, I think, be all that more adept, attuned to what matters as they play in our grownup world.

February 2022

## On Holiday

From our perch beside the Ionian Sea,

We jousted over "sea" and "ocean."

I called the expanse of water that glittered beyond us, "ocean."

Jean said "sea."

Which was the encompassing phenomenon, I asked.

Which the broader definition?

Couldn't one be the other?

Poets employed them interchangeably, I said.

Turns out, once sailors traveled far enough to name the expanses of water over which they voyaged,

Once geographers parsed the information that sailors brought from a round and buxom globe,

The two became distinct.

A sea the smaller body of water, with land arms embracing it.

Not a lake held hostage to a shore,

Not the unbound infinity of an ocean either.

But a baby ocean wrapped in the earth's hug.

Poets were, perhaps, lazy, or, as always, hunting for synonyms.

~ ~ ~

So, we were on holiday beside the Ionian Sea.

On holiday? Another mystery.

When I was a child, we took vacations—my dad escaping the confines and discomfitures of work.

Vacating his desk at the Farmer's Alliance, our car pointed to Iowa and Indiana, to relatives and friends.

An escape, a recess, time "off."

And holidays, in my youth, single days. National commemorations, food and family; no work or school; though chores figured prominently too: the garage swept, leaves raked, ledgers balanced.

But here, beside the Ionian Sea, I wasn't on vacation or honoring a hero.

I was, with Bryan and Jean, on holiday.

Not just time away—but time for sandcastles and deck chairs and umbrellas and tea, for cottages and collections of shells.

For lazing, letting go, carrying on—for leaving behind not just "home" but the cautions and constraints of daily life.

For celebrating seasides, mountain streams, rugged hillsides pinned to the earth by gnarled olive trees.

Worlds in which to lounge and laugh, tan, trek, linger over a coffee, learn.

For abandoning news and regimented time.

For giggling.

For encouraging conversation to take scenic routes and obscure byways and come back to the respect and comfort of friendship.

For allowing the waves of our shared days to dazzle in sun... and sea... and memory.

October 2021

## Two Weeks on Wineham Lane...

Which is a mid-sized rural road linking Cowfold Road/ A272 and the Henfield/ Wheatsheaf Road in West Sussex. And West Sussex is, as you likely know, a British county (once a shire) in be-tween London and Brighton. My friends Bryan and Jean live on Wineham Lane in Royal Oak Country Park. And with much love and cre-ativity provided their home and their hospitality for those weeks.

Yes, I was on Wineham Lane during King Charles III's coronation. Jean and Bryan had hung bunting and the Union Jack and the Stars and Stripes and had planted flowers in red, white, and blue along their porch. We glued ourselves to the TV during the procession from Buckingham Palace to Westminster and back to the balcony waving. And the next day, Sunday, the residents of Royal Oak Country Park held a small soiree to celebrate: treats, decorations, games, and a toast to their new monarch. After that, news of the Coronation revolved mostly around the question of whether Princess Anne's military plume was situated deliberately, directly in front of Harry. Four days later, when Jean and I sampled London, we didn't see or hear evidence of an earth-shattering event. Daily life in Britain seemed to just pick up and go on.

When I left Montana on May first, the land between my windows and the mountains was still beige. Buds on our deciduous trees hesitated to open. Grass had just begun to perk up. Despite a few warm days, April had treated us to two batches of heavy wet snow and some incidental flurries. We were a child's brown-outlined coloring page waiting to be filled in.

I'd visited Jean and Bryan before. But this time, with spring arriving in full measure there, I reveled in a land suffused with green and birdsong. Giant, twisted oaks framing the sky. Tunnels of newly-leafed trees arching over country lanes. Seen from Devil's Dyke, the South Downs stretching out in bright green and yellow—grass and rapeseed. Ivy and holly climbing up and over walls, trees, light posts, whole houses. Mama sheep and cavorting lambs—outlined against long lush meadows. Gorse bushes fading from gold blooms to green. Fields of bluebells along the roads. Jean and Bryan's secret garden fresh, flourishing, lush. And there, especially there, birds singing. Not just the chirping or cawing of my neighborhood. But floating melodies and trills out over the park. I'd come to an aviary, it seemed.

I welcomed every errand that Bryan and Jean needed to run around Sussex. It's a land of ancient lanes linked by roundabouts with cars and buses and lorries shooting off into one exit or another. To villages—jewel after jewel of small, old settlements. My memory is alight in narrow high streets lined with this rich spill of historic buildings: half-timbered, medieval, Victorian, Tudor, Sussex flint. Busy with real shops—green grocers, bakeries, charity, pubs. Buildings that have been used for hundreds of years—still serving their little settlements: flats above, commerce on the street. Ditchling, Wineham and Twineham, Steyning, Henfield, Upper Beeding, Hurstpierpoint, Small Dole, Cuckfield.

I close my eyes and compare that abundance, that profusion, that extravagance of historic structures to Montana's tiny towns. In which we celebrate the survival of a 1910 one-roomed frame school or an abandoned brick corner homestead bank. Or fawn over mining ghost towns—the black ribs of their rafters outlined against our big sky. Two worlds where our differences in history and population density and commerce and governing loom large even when we speak many of the same words.

My visit included a trip to Arundel Castle—an 11th century complex much modified over the years, especially in the 19th century. A property of the Dukes of Norfolk since the 1500s. Everything any British aficionado would want in a castle: gardens and keeps and moats and great rooms and chapels, armouries, a portcullis, coats of arms, statuary and portraits. Everything but a dungeon—though maybe that was just left out of the tour.

Jean and I took the train to London. And a boat along the Thames to see the city from the waterway that has drawn humans to this metropolis for at least 2,000 years. Wharves, warehouses turned fancy homes, mudlarking visitors, and ancient pubs lining the river in front of steeples and skyscrapers. Every bridge had its own story—including one I'd never heard: that during World War II, homebound women finished construction of the Waterloo Bridge—now the Ladies' Bridge. After lunch in Greenwich—the place on earth from which we measure time and distance—an ordinary taxi ride back to Bankside served up another magic feast for my eyes and imagination.

Jean and Bryan have tolerated my weak knees on previous trips to Wineham Lane and other European posts. But those knees proved especially vexing and wearisome this time around. They required—really I required—extra arms and handholds. Jean and Bryan made so much possible.

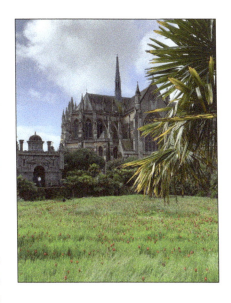

This was our "Wisteria Visit." Early on, as we walked the Arundel gardens, we realized that the draping vines of purple flowers weren't lilacs. And for an afternoon, the three of us couldn't summon the name. Once we held the word on our tongues, we found that wisteria cascaded down many walls and buildings. Our eyes were drawn to it. "In the language of flowers, it [wisteria] says youth, poetry and 'Let's Be Friends.'" Originally from Asia, Europeans cultivated it.

Victorians especially prized wisteria and offered it to others to say "I cling to you" as it would cling to the branches of other trees. Ironically, most all of the plant is poisonous. Work that out!!

Maybe the contradiction between flowery meanings and toxicity isn't as unusual as it seems at first blush. As you know, all travel is complicated: it's adventure we seek and dream about; it's the weariness and challenges of unfamiliar places and customs; it's realities that enchant and disappoint. It brings sweet companionship, the opportunity to meet new and fascinating people, and a particular loneliness—for me, the quiet and cat-filled world of my daily life. Still, here, back in Montana, I'll take the beauty of wisteria and the enticements of travel. And the sumptuous British spring—even as I navigate it on creaky knees.

May 2023

# THIS CLOSING SEASON

*Today, I sat down with the surgeon who's about to replace both my knees. Young, terse, all business, good answers to my first questions. He did not sugarcoat the pain; he's using a spinal not general anesthesia—my preference too; he promised that the new knee and its connections would be solid—no chance for hurting the work. Apart from pain and stiffness, I could move as I chose. "Really," I said. And then, from some quirky corner of my brain, I blathered on, "oh that means I can feed the cats and clean their litter." And I'd just lost every bit of credibility—cachet—I might have had. Dr. S. rolled his eyes at the even younger man taking notes. They were laughing among themselves around the desk when I left.*

*Like many older folks, I spend a good swatch of time with other seniors in offices: the ophthalmologist, the audiologist, orthopedists, physical therapists. I shop when my peers shop. And to a person, we all try to fudge on our age. I am not about to dye my hair blonde and try to look 50. But secretly I would like folks to think I'm 65 (that occurred a dozen years ago). Which—even if the doctor had not read the paperwork—I blew with my mention of cats.*

*You will already have read this acknowledgement in the previous batch of essays: "So I am one more old lady who loves her cats." The heart of that sentence is simply that I am an old woman. And as billions of folks before me know, being that isn't easy. There are hundreds of pithy quotations on the topic—none of which obliterate the truths: we are lucky to still be here; all the vitamins and exercise in the world will not buy us a one-way ticket to the Fountain of Youth; at varying rates, we will lose—a body that we can take for granted, our colleagues and friends, our capacity to make more marks in the world, some or all of our memories, ourselves.*

*Which means that we damn well better embrace our quirks—our observations—every tender moment—every sunset—very song—every pet that brings us joy. Never mind how odd or pathetic the youngsters in our lives see us.*

*In this next set of essays, you'll find me trying to reach beyond the losses of this closing season to the life I can live now.*

## Coming to Terms...

With life running out.

My own. And so many others. Bob, Tony Incashola, Ian Tyson, Chuck Johnson, Kay Flinn, Connie Waterman. Before that Ivan and Kay Rosengren and Dick Ensminger and Gene over in Harlowton and Jean and Clarence. Before that Dave. My folks. George and Dorothy. Big Marcella. Harry Pfanz. Lee Lengel. Tom Govan, Gary, Barb, the entire panoply of aunts and uncles and the honorary McPherson ones.

The relentless march of loss—of watching the people who defined my life, steadied it, brought joy to it, leave. Not just watching. Feeling. Emptiness. Disbelief. Rebellion.

Until at last, I look at myself—in the context of those departed and those frail ones further along on their trips.

Which means coming to terms with my own knees and legs—the annoying, wearying, limiting debilities that leave me moving slowly and carefully.

Coming to terms with all that I won't do again. The places that I won't go. The exhilaration of accomplishments and invested skill unlikely to be ahead.

Coming to terms with an increasingly dated knowledge of historic preservation and Montana. Two generations behind already.

Coming to terms with being an antique. A relic from a time whose customs and belongings are quaint, old-fashioned.

I write—I suspect—as a cry to the universe to say: NOT ME. HOW HAS IT COME TO THIS FOR MEEEEEEEEEEEEEE!

Believing, as did my dad though for different reasons, that I can outwit this stage of life.

Surely if I find a goal, a special project, the right words, I'll escape. For now at least.

Or, if all women's magazine and AARP's articles are to be believed, bravely facing forward, adopting the right diet and wardrobe and chair exercises. Just plain denying reality—for as long as that trick works.

But I live grieving. The losses are real. I am not fantasizing what will not return and will not happen.

The fact of the matter—the plain reality—is I am returning to the ether, the universe, back to energy.

What remains is living the last chapter. Maybe engaged in the last stories with energy and enthusiasm. Or, if it comes to that, living the frightening, ugly, drooling, incontinent, wheelchair goodbye.

But living. Until I'm not.

Always always doing what I can. Relishing what I can in words and friendships and skies and art and warmth and cats and hugs and memories. And gratitude.

To waste no hours feeling put upon or martyred or singled out. To spare the world false bravado. To grieve but not wallow.

To know, instead, empathy and curiosity and—as every self-help book and mantra advises:  acceptance.

**April 2023**

## Lament

I come to this winter season—this icy interlude of cold and snow and thin light—lonely. I am struck by the yawning emptinesses once filled by friends and family and colleagues who are now gone. This year most especially Connie and Tony and Bob. Their time and place in my life differed enormously. I cherished each of them in their own important way.

Their "passings"—an intriguing word that begs the question of "to where"—follows many others. A panoply of the people who I have loved and respected. A chorus, a troupe, an aggregate of folks who defined my choices and opportunities and tastes: Dave; my parents; Dave's parents; the two history profs who illumined the past; Mike and Helen; Pearl and Delbert; the Sundquists; Alice and Lew; Don and Big Marcella; Ivan; Kermit and Edith; Walter and Merle; Lynn Hafermehl; Kay; Gary; all my dad and mother's siblings; Dr. Pfanz; Flossie and Lavina and Jessie. I feel a peace in naming the ones I can remember.

Fewer and fewer people who've carried me through life—with whom I've shared ideas and dinners and pranks and beauty and tears—are alive to keep me in their thoughts. However long in the past some of my friendships, those folks once experienced a small electrical pulse at the word "Marcella." Not necessarily accurate or affectionate. Nor deep or considered. But I existed—we all exist—for a while in the synapses of those we know. We are known—physically and in the grid systems of each other's brains and heart. But as we age, as our friends age, our worlds and minds quiet. The living array of people within my circuitry has surely diminished. And I am, especially in this dark season, left desolate by the hollows, the chimeras, once occupied by beloved folks now gone.

When I conjure Connie and Tony and Bob, I see their silhouettes. Not their faces now. But their outlines. The space they occupied in this world. In my world. And it's that frame, that vacuum, that haunts me. That yawning emptiness that proves their absence but still carries their shape. They have become the unfaded squares of wallpaper where pictures once hung. Noticeable by their removal.

Only yesterday, it seems, I shared opinions and observations and laughter with Connie. I heard her voice, blossomed with her caring, and celebrated the opportunities that came my way to share my respect and joy for her. To experience the electrical frisson that was CONNIE! And know that Connie felt that same jolt, that rush of memory and feeling when she thought of me. And we were substance! We could begin and end our visits by hugging each other.

Instead, her outline, the physical space she occupied in our universe is deserted and unoccupied. And the sparks of mind and heart that animated her seem stilled.

There's a question, of course, that we rarely entertain in polite society: What about ghosts? What about spirits? Is there more energy, more qu'i nestled within those floating outlines than we acknowledge. Souls, maybe? Should we look more diligently or wait more expectantly? Are we less alone than we believe? Who knows?

Grief exists for all sentient beings, I believe. It has shadowed life far longer than I can imagine. It has been sung and painted and shaped into words and molded into clay from time immemorial. Eloquently. Evocatively. Radiantly. I claim no prowess, no artistry in wrestling with loss. Just loneliness. And a commitment to remembering. To flooding those outlines with the stories and images that still fire in my brain—as long as I can.

December 2022

## An App for This Age

Awhile back, I downloaded the phone app "We Croak." It's based on a Bhutanese belief that to live fully we must contemplate death often. Become its friend. Five times daily at random moments the app pops up with quotations to spur such thoughts.

But contemplating death is not, I believe, the discipline I most need. Instead, I need an app called "I Fail" or "I Decline." And quotes that offer clear-eyed words about the next chapter of my life. What advancing years are wont to bring. Wise sayings not about mortality but about our bodies' and minds' deterioration. And how we might live those dim and waning times.

That is, after all, what my friends and I talk about. We speculate about our acquaintances and the thin line on which they teeter between independence and reliance on others. That no man's land between familiar routines, even those that are getting more difficult and chancy, and the land of the very old—the dependent, the vulnerable.

We sound supportive as we gossip. We tut. And shake our heads. We see the coming disasters so clearly. One fall. One loss of caregivers. One turn into confusion. And we anticipate—for our friends, of course, and with some righteousness—the much-dreaded outcomes: a move to Ascension Retreat, Holiday Haven, Life Care Gardens, Autumn Acres, Harbor Village, Touchstone Ranch. The cunningly named purgatories further defined by slickly warm adjectives: gracious, active, homey, cozy.

But WE, WE are good at buzzing along, adapting, trimming our expectations, pulling in our horns, making do. We attempt to exercise and eat and read ourselves into stasis. We try the panaceas that doctors and AARP offer. We've done our best to sort belongings and write wills. We aren't foolhardy about these next years.

But neither are we especially realistic.

We anticipate some outside assistance. We see our spare rooms as homes for a grateful, helpful college student or a young retiree who could look in on us. We think our money might just stretch for home health aides. Our friends have said: call me if you need a hand. Our children may be close by. We know, vaguely, that our community offers meals on wheels and bus service.

There is, of course, always the off chance that we will die quickly and without fuss. At home. But two-thirds of us won't. We will have moved or "been put" into one form or another of an institution.

So what do we do? What do I do? I've spent longer thinking about that than applying words to this page. And still suspect that I must dig much deeper.

But first, albeit with some reluctance, I'm inclined to think that keeping more fit than I am is a grand idea. No guarantees, but why invite trouble. Then I suspect, I should sort more—dive into the trunks and drawers that hold what I couldn't give away a year or so ago and purge again. And keep doing that.

Then, then I think I need to live lightly, thankfully. To savor today's gifts more than I do now. And to understand that the heart of this world's sweetness lies in people and pets and words and art and music. To recognize that every day brings me a concert and an art gallery and a classic and love. If I look for them. If I choose to accept their presence. It isn't just martyrdom or downcast acceptance. It is—in its own way—just seeing what is and being grateful for it. I discovered this past week, for example, that the Chevy dealership's rainbow of helium balloons makes me uncommonly happy. And two new kittens may not be wise additions to my 75-year-old-life. But we each thrive on the other's love!

Next, I'm considering my own time as daughter and daughter-in-law. Meal maker. Caregiver. Arranger. When the tables are turned, I want to accept that assistance with nothing but a glad and contented heart and tongue. Our children and our friends haven't really factored our dependency into their mid-life agendas.

And if or when I need an institutional purgatory, I must accept that decline and debility is as much a part of life as birth and death. And that our purgatories are palaces compared to where most of the world's citizens live.

Along the way, I might be wise to picture those final months or years baldly. Look unflinchingly at the realities of incontinence, inactivity, dementia, fear. I might escape, but then again I might not.

So let my Apple watch buzz. Let my "I Fail" app ding. I think it says:

*"The thing about growing old is you have to accept it—if you don't, you'll be as miserable as sin. You've got to try and find the few good things about it."* -Judy Parfitt

**August 2022**

## A Prescription for Our Fears

Grandma Sherfy was my current age—75—in 1963.

That year, I was a cocky high school junior—finding my bearings, myself, my prowess.

Aunt Blanche would die in November—breast cancer.

So would President Kennedy.

We were catching our breath on the far side of the Cuban missile crisis.

Grandma would live another decade.

And in that time, she worried about many things.

Where would the money come from? Widowed young, always a homemaker and a preacher's wife, she had no financial resources.

Could she still babysit or care for the more frail?

How much would she have to depend on my dad and mom?

Had her children married well?

How often would she have to put up with Aunt Mary?

Was her church becoming too liberal, too worldly?

She was often unsettled, aggrieved, dour. She was the "hard" grandma—whose nineteenth century corset made it difficult to exchange affectionate hugs. She fretted over much that she could not relinquish to her god in spite of his promises.

But—of all that troubled her—dementia was not on her list.

It is on mine—and those of my contemporaries.

The horrifying, unthinkable, numerically-all-too-probable possibility of ceasing to know reality;

Or ourselves

And all that we love—family and friends and books and memories and place.

It is the torment of aging in this century; the most dire of diagnoses.

It's rendered cancer and heart disease reassuring.

And it niggles at the edge of our everyday lives:

> Keys stowed in the wrong pocket of my purse;
>
> Emails repeated within the same hour to the same recipient;
>
> A familiar face hanging there with no name;
>
> Sour cream purchased twice in one week.

We let none of those moments slide by us without the question.

Without the fear.

And so we let worry become its own truth. Its own disease.

PhDs and MDs speculate about this pandemic of dementia.

Is it because we live longer?

Or that they've tamed other old people ailments?

Is it our toxic world?

It's all speculation.

And the recommended nostrums offered for every element of aging: to exercise, eat well, be social, be mellow.

In fact, magazines should no longer accept chirpy cure-all articles that feature those panaceas. We know. God we know!

I, for one, though, think that our **fear of dementia** should itself be a condition. A diagnosis. A disease to address.

And that our doctors should write this prescription:

*Play, eat what you want, sing off key, wiggle your butt when your favorite music comes along, leave the bed unmade and your towel on the bathroom floor at least once a week.*

*Sit on your porch as the sun comes down in the summer. Follow the trill of a robin at dusk and a magpie's gossip. Let your dog and cat snuggle into bed with you.*

*Read. Find eloquence in poems and essays and mysteries and rom coms. Write. Paint. Cook. Garden.*

*Above all, surround yourself with people who laugh and who treasure every element of the world's splendor and silliness.*

*Of course, contribute—share a bit of your muscle and intellect and caring with others. Nothing huge—just something real.*

And then, in the event that the universe slips in to borrow a bit of your memory before you're ready, you'll be caught unawares. Maybe singing and dancing and laughing. Maybe the plague of panic and despair won't have cheated you of precious hours.

May 2022

## In Memoriam

*I am what time, circumstance, history, have made of me, certainly, but I am, also, much more than that.*
*So are we all. -James Baldwin*

I once read obits more carefully, for the stories they told. To absorb the reality that these were busy, distinct, fulsome lives. That are now gone forever. And in the leaving have taken with them entire encyclopedias of knowledge and memory and feeling. That not just the person—a name—is gone, but the whole of their skills and experiences.

I haven't abandoned that sacrament,

But now I look first to see whether the newly-dead were younger or older than I am.

And take a minute to put myself in context. Or try.

But all too often, I am impatient with the formulaic tales that death notices tell.

The dead married the love of their lives, their soulmates—usually the second time around. Having made some serious (but obviously unexplained) mistakes the first time.

More than their children, they doted on their grandchildren.

Who adored their baking and their homemade afghans. Nannie or Ompa were just the best.

They made every holiday special.

They loved the great outdoors. They could fix anything.

They were selfless; they volunteered; they were cheerful in the face of hardship.

They fought a lengthy, brave battle against the illness that killed them.

They died with their family gathered round.

The doors of heaven opened and they have enjoyed a warm reunion with parents.

Right.

~ ~ ~

Dave, you may remember, launched "Speaking Ill of the Dead: Jerks in Montana History" as an antidote to the hero-worshippers who haunted the Historical Society library.

The relatives who arrived eager to read up on grandpa's small-town stardom: sheriff or legislator; banker or Exalted Elk.

The family was startled to find that their beloved ancestor faced prison time or bankruptcy. Or died in the county poor farm (yes, they existed).

A decade after immersing himself in Montana records and newspapers, Dave recognized realities for what they were: that no one escapes this life with a clean slate; that the colorful characters whom descendants hoped to celebrate were often rascals. Or human.

*The town father who kept his Blackfeet wife in a cabin behind his elegant bungalow.*

*The senators who voted to imprison German speakers during World War I.*

*The industrious miners and their bosses who visited Venus Alley, Butte's red light district.*

*The community leaders who appeared on small town 1920s Ku Klux Klan rolls.*

*The Butte physician, Fascist, nudist-colony proprietor elected to Congress—briefly.*

*The businessmen who expanded their holdings—a lot—during the Depression.*

So I read Sunday's obits in our diminutive newspaper with a grain of salt.

And in the way of most seniors, feel a bit of relief that at 75, I am still here. Even though I need all the help I can get to navigate stairs.

But I am eager to find an honest summary of someone's life: she always cooked Thanksgiving dinner and everyone avoided her gravy; she was pregnant with little Robbie when they got married; he couldn't hold a job for more than a year—that sharp tongue of his got him in trouble; of course she adapted to the outdoors—that cabin on Flathead Lake was a disaster; she held that position for 40 years because childraising wasn't her forte; she hated sports; he hated movies; he hit her; she had an affair.

We are a bundle of untold stories, of truths that we hope will never surface. Of truths, the whole of which imbue us with color and fire and intricacy. Which, in the end, award us our humanity, give us all three dimensions.

Historians approach written records skeptically—especially obits. They know to match record against record: to run our lives through the sieves of city directories and birth certificates, police files, transcripts, report cards, oral histories when enough time has passed that the interviewee won't fudge.

To recognize obituaries for what they are: those first full grieving outcries; those faltering attempts to piece the family together; that all-too-human hankering to shine a precious light on our closest relatives—at least for public consumption.

So now, here in this Monday morning quiet, you should know that I was Dave's fourth wife. I was never his soulmate. I think that high school girlfriend Lola qualified on that front. That it was my gravy that never passed muster; Dave encouraged me to use those little envelopes of powered mix instead. That I quit balancing my checkbook a year or so ago in absolute defiance of my dad. That yes, being a stepmom was hard. That I had little courage for dealing with difficult employees. I wanted to keep everyone happy. To no one's benefit. That my Covid 20 pounds can all be ascribed to donuts and frosted sugar cookies. That for many DC years I hid the gin from my visiting parents. That my sartorial extravagances revolve around shoes for my gnarled feet. I'd rather you didn't pray for me. Although I know that prayer's innocuous, its framework so often isn't. That I never stay in touch with friends the way I intend. That I so know better, but continue to love Montana and hate her winters.

That's maybe a first taste of honesty. Maybe enough for the newspaper to lift me out of clichés. But, of course, you likely know much more!

**April 2022**

## Wanting

This early spring, I stretched to the far side of my memory,

Stalking riches: the pure gold of so many moments that life has given me;

The uncanny, dazzling opportunities that I never saw coming in my Kansas growing up.

And I fell into a loneliness, a grief, a longing so sharp I couldn't swallow.

I wanted back in my green pencil skirt at Gettysburg.

I wanted to walk for the first time ever into the Interior Building, knowing I belonged.

I wanted the improbable moment at Dulles when Bob welcomed a ride home.

I wanted oysters on the half shell and a Manhattan, the sweet comfort of a Saturday night stretched along his lap, hearing Bernard DeVoto lead us cross country.

I wanted the beginnings of a new job, the shivery amalgam of fear and confidence;

And the rush of telling preservation stories.

I wanted Ian Tyson summoning love.

And then Rodney singing joy.

I wanted to drive five hours to the North Fork and know that Dave would be alone, working in the meadow, impatient to see me.

I wanted the ferry ride to Patmos and the vaporetto trip around Venice and Carrara's marble canyons and London's improbable Underground.

I wanted to meet these mountains again as new friends and to see the Big Sky's incomparable blue for the first time, the limitless home to which I now belonged.

Foolishly, futilely I wanted...

I traded gratitude for grief

And melancholy.

And the dense weight of age.

Where once the world had leaned down and stretched its hours out and lovingly placed the next adventure into my arms,

Now I hear the doors to times past, to new geographies, to changing careers snick shut quietly and firmly.

Except, of course, we know the answer—at least on sunny days:

We are never without the treasure chest of this moment.

And if, as is the truth, the next exploits are more ethereal, more emotional, more intimate, they remain new territory. Unexplored. Rugged. Singular.

Literally life and death.

**April 2022**

## Birds of a Feather

Yesterday, I stood and watched a magpie winkling bites from the suet feeder,

Which hangs off my porch rail—made fetching by a tin beak, tail, painted wings, and the wire feet of a northern flicker. (I had to look that up on Google.)

I watch often. And now that we have snow, I watch for the dainty footsteps of visiting birds and the peripatetic tail swishes of a squirrel.

I offer sunflower seeds and three kinds of suet and a heated birdbath/drinking fountain.

Risking multicolored plops of poop on the white railings.

All new for me this year.

I am so not a birder.

I maybe recognize half a dozen species and guess at the rest.

I'm a fool for robins—and the songs they sing from summer treetops at the edge of night.

I risk driving off highways to follow hawks riding the air and eyeing gophers.

Ian Tyson long since sealed my enchantment with magpies:

*Magpie*
*You're an early riser*
*Magpie*
*You're a bold chastiser*
*Magpie*
*Always waking up my wife and I*
*You old coyote in the sky*
*Magpie*
*Some say you're a bold deceiver*
*I say you're a true believer*

*Magpie*
*You know the west ain't never going*
*to die*
*Just as long as you can fly*

So, I am uncommonly pleased, surprised, touched to watch a magpie just feet from my own warm inside perch.

To feel as if he's come to visit **me**.

And then a faraway memory of the Grandma Kitty Christmas story floats to the surface. Grandma Kitty being Dave's grandmother.

She sometimes lived with Dave's family, but more often stayed in a Wisconsin old folks' home.

The family regularly failed to think up good Christmas gift ideas. She needed nothing, really.

But outside her rest home room they'd hung a bird feeder.

So, Eureka, bird seed!

Which meant that one Christmas she unwrapped not one but four or five bags of bird seed from under the Christmas tree. Each giver unaware of the others' choice.

Dave told the story with laughter—like that of the family as Grandma Kitty unveiled one sack of seed after another.

I may have become Grandma Kitty.

I don't need much of anything in the way of earthly goods. In fact, I keep winnowing belongings. Not perhaps, to nursing home constraints, but for sure to honor these small spaces.

My life is more circumscribed, too, cautious. Do I honestly want to run errands in the snow, wobbly and timid as I am in these Covid times?

So yes, I love to see the world from my window.

And escape my four walls on the wings of a mischievous magpie and the life I imagine he lives in our big sky.

To glow in the satisfaction of being a worthy host to a friend so exotic.

**December 2021**

## The Competition

No one talks about it.

The topic being too close to home.

A guilty secret.

But, I bet, if you're over 65 you know...

That we are racing each other away from the threshold of death.

Backpedaling for all we're worth.

Subtly. Surreptitiously.

Avoiding garish makeup or bad dye jobs or clothes too young for us.

We're not denying our age.

Just trying to rebrand ourselves a bit.

If 50 is the new 40, we're working hard to make 80 the new 65.

Which is a "cool" age—an "on the cusp" age.

We're working to flaunt our fitness and tout our trips.

To discount whatever small trauma took us to the emergency room.

Or reduce say, by half, our prescriptions, when asked.

And leave out a fall or two on our Medicare questionnaire—it's no one's business anyway.

And fill our vocabulary with verbs that haven't been relevant for a decade: dash, pop over, whip up, scurry, run by, sprint.

We're competing in this reverse age contest not for our children or our young friends.

They've seen us as old for a long time now.

We're contending with each other.

We've exhausted most of the other fields of competition in which we once engaged.

Salaries, titles, travels, children's achievements, grandchildren's charms, hobbies, do-gooding—you know.

So here we are (don't tell me I'm the only one!):

I know I'm old. And you are too.

But grace and vigor, fearlessness, relevance are the qualities to project.

The façade to maintain with our contemporaries.

To be the Homecoming Queens of Aging High.

Old but not decaying.

Old but managing.

Old but graceful.

Fit old. Engaged old.

Purposeful.

And to state the obvious, the game has a conclusion.

You lose when you die.

For all the honest grief we feel when a good friend passes on,

For all the new and real loneliness we experience,

For all the chill that scurries up our spines, knowing we are that much closer.

We feel a furtive, illicit quiver of pleasure:  we won.

**Postscript.**

I was home in Kansas to visit my dad a month before he died. We'd called in hospice. He needed to move from assisted living to nursing home care, and he was having none of it. He was scared and angry. He seemed to be considering death honestly, personally, for the first time in his life. And was quite startled and upset that all his years of church work and pious deprivation hadn't paid off in immortality. But what he said at one point tipped me off to this essay:  his lifelong rival, the thorn in his side in Kiwanis, in church, in our small college doings was going to outlive him.

November 2021

## I Learned This Year...

More about growing old and navigating the world.

I am 75.

And tentative, slow on steps, unsteady on rocky ground. More so after a silly, spectacular sprawl in my living room last spring. The perfect example of senior magazines' warnings:  tripping on a rug.

I rise up from squishy chairs only if they have sturdy arms.

Child-height toilets are the death of me.

I hear the world with my right ear—and not my left, at all.

And require my right ear to keep me steady, balanced.

The ophthalmologist and I hold macular degeneration at bay.

My gray hair's gone white in these pandemic times.

But...

I stay busy and write pieces like this and keep my finances in order and remember a host of birthdays and how to order groceries. I can arrange Zoom meetings and chair them. Book travel and unsnarl some of my computer's quirks. Now that they all talk, I can mind grandchildren for a bit. And cook for company. So far, I haven't left my car keys in the freezer. Though I empathize with anyone who has.

Still, I welcome a clear-voiced speaker.

I treasure handrails and grab bars and gentle slopes.

I'm Marcella or Mrs. Walter.

Please not sweetie or hon (as a physician's assistant regretted saying earlier this year).

I thrive on matter-of-fact thoughtfulness (don't we all).

I can use an arm for steadiness sometimes, not always. I'll ask.

Or you can offer.

But I'm not anyone's dependent.

I don't benefit from hovering or scolding or presuming or being corrected.

I'm self-conscious enough.

And very much my own person.

Of greatest importance: needing help sometimes doesn't mean I'm helpless.

I'm responsible, as well, for accepting assistance with grace and dignity. With thanks, but not apology.

I look ahead beyond 75 and know that the intertwined graces of mutual respect become more important every passing year.

That the aides and nurses and doctors and friends and children in my future might benefit from every flicker of this rumination.

As will I. As will I.

November 2021

## Things I Don't Understand...

It's a long list.

And begins with—well, I don't even have a name for it. Not just technology. Not just a cloud. Not electrical currents. "IT" delivers all the information and pictures and video and sound that pop out of my laptop and screen. Seemingly transported by nothing but air. What do we call that? And how the hell does it happen.

Or bitcoin? I'm still back in early Cro-Magnon time hoping that there's gold underground at Fort Knox. One ounce of gold for every paper dollar I have. I know that we're long beyond that. But I just don't understand when we shifted over to play money. Never mind that now even more ephemeral "dollars" are "mined" somewhere— but don't exist. How the hell does bitcoin contribute to global warming if it's AWOL?

Which makes non-fungible tokens an even greater mystery. I kind of get the idea that humans have decided that intangible feelings have value. Of course they do. But in what universe do we need to give them financial value? You mean, I could have "sold" the love I felt for Dave to someone else if I had kept a decent ledger of how I loved him every day. If I had had a block-chain documenting that love.

Hell, yes, I use Google to try to understand all this. And one term at a time, I think I get the gist. But when I put them together, I am confused, stupefied, at sea.

Let's not even talk about A.I. and ChatGPT. Once more, I

understand that we first feared and then indeed discovered that all the little motherboards in our computers had—without our telling them to—outgrown us. Had learned to think and reason and make connections on their own. I know for a fact that when I play Scrabble on my computer, the computer has "learned" better and better strategies to beat me. Mimicking my own moves. It's only held back by my telling it to be "easy" on me. We're in the realm of science fiction here—especially the early sci-fi horror stories that sprang up long before a computer outplayed everyone on Jeopardy.

I don't understand how we ever transport enough food into New York or Seattle or Los Angeles to feed the MILLIONS of mouths there. Here in Helena, I see the Albertsons' semis pull into the delivery slots at Safeway. But for millions of people? There must be hundreds of thousands of trucks pulling in and out 24 hours a day to multiple docks. The city streets have to be clogged with trucks.

And then, there's the garbage. Here in Helena, I know it's Monday morning when I hear the city truck come, emit its back-up beeps and scoop up the big green dumpsters at the apartment complex next door. And, like all Helenans, I take my glass and plastics to the adroitly named "transfer station" and see the yawning abyss into which the dump trucks deposit garbage. But for millions?? I can't get my mind around it.

And when I take the last size XL Time and True jeggings off the rack at Walmart, how does it happen that several new pairs of XL Time and True jeggings are located in China, placed in a huge container with hundreds of unrelated products, transported across the Pacific, and put on the right semi in Long Beach and delivered to Helena. It's unfathomable.

And, in a different vein, I cannot imagine what workers around the world think or feel as they manufacture enough glitter-laden ribbon, ornaments, wreaths, greeting cards, and fake Christmas trees for us. First off, all that glitter has to be a serious health hazard. And for sure, it's as wasteful and unneeded as a product could be. Now here the web did me some good. Cleopatra made glitter out of crushed up beetles. Ours is usually a combination of aluminum and polyethylene terephthalate (PET). Makes you feel really fine about wearing makeup full of glitter!

I'm just as perplexed about our priorities. Since acquiring Tiger Tiger and Tuxedo, I have purchased an obscene number of clever cat toys. Snakes that crawl across the floor, eyes flashing and forked tongues darting in and out. Packages of what I call "bice"—little fuzzy objects shaped like mice but with bird feathers attached. The ultimate fantasy for indoor cats. How is it that we slide farther and farther away from world peace or nuclear disarmament agreements but keep designing and making better and better cat toys?

Or guns. Or gummies for every single human ailment. Or wicked apps with games that involve as much death as possible. Or purple fake fingernails that last for weeks.

And I have no way of understanding why one or two people choose to build and live in a house with 15 bedrooms and 20 bathrooms. Or wear "couture" dresses that cost $10,000. I mean, what's the joy in that except to brag about its NFTs—non-fungible tokens. Envy, in other words, if I'm on the right track.

And why do so many new cars look either like hearses or like someone accidently poured a bucket of mud into the paint before it was sprayed on.

Why do the new credit unions and churches in Helena have interchangeable, nonsensical names: Intrepid Credit Union, Ascent Bank, Narrate Church, Life Church, Fresh Life Church, Well Church, Vocal Credit Union, Opportunity Bank. Why not the Opportunity Church or the Intrepid Congregation. I swear every time I go by one of the billboards hawking these institutions I have a conversation with myself: "Of course, I would like my bank account to ascend, but I bet you aren't promising that." "And why would I seek out a vocal credit union, unless that's a promise to let a real person answer my call, rather than an automated voice."

A few of the sturdy old names remain: United Methodist and Bank of the Rockies. But none have the cachet of the oh-so-secure Pioneer Savings and Loan Association that held my childhood account.

Of course, if I happen to love a mystery product, I'm not as cynical. Take e-readers for instance. The fact that I can travel to Europe with a library of a couple thousand books at my fingerprints and still meet weight limits is purely miraculous. But how is it that we haven't made e-readers and millions of age-appropriate books available to children around the globe in all languages. We could, I believe.

Twentieth-century Marcella understood a lot of our world. Not everything. But I could see how a correcting Selectric typewriter worked. I learned about what keeps airplanes aloft. I "got" penicillin—as a miracle mold. The cats of my youth played with grocery bags and string—and real birds. Telephone lines and electric wires were visible. Accurate or not, I could picture little bursts of current or sound scooting along them. Grandpa Pyle gave us real silver dollars for our birthdays.

I'm saying nothing at all, really, except that I'm old. Except that I'm less attuned to the changes in our world. Retiring truly brought cataclysmic change to my knowledge and life. Nothing now requires me to understand the contemporary world easily—fluidly. While it is second nature to my 50-year-old-nephews.

But I do want to stay curious. To know enough to want to know more. To cozy up to—rather than shy away from—the vocabulary and images and worries and possibilities of these years—not just the ones of 50 years ago.

For no other reason than that a complex universe is more wondrous to consider. Or that inquiring minds have all the fun!

**April 2023**

## Bonus Time

Growing up, "bonus" meant the red tin of fruitcake that my dad received at Christmas from the Farmer's Alliance boss. Every year. Without fail. No one in our family savored fruitcake. But no one in our family threw away food either. So Mother engineered thin little slices to eat with ice cream or to serve Mrs. Kubin with Monday morning coffee.

I liked the tins with their old-fashioned pictures—a cowboy roping, a stately white house with a horse and carriage in front and a Victorian couple walking through the snow. Holly at the bottom. Company president E. C. Mingenback (you'll remember that my sister and I referred to him as Mr. Stingyback) bought the tins in bulk from the Collin Street Bakery in Corsicana, Texas, for all the men. Not the hourly-wage "girls."

Given what we all thought of fruitcake and given the stress and distress that our dad experienced in his working world, those tins did not seem like bonuses. They were an insult, a taunt, the most ungenerous of thank-yous. My dad deserved much more.

The Latin ancestor of "bonus" is literally "good." Its cousin is "bounty." And we use those words to define payment beyond what is expected, a gift, a perk, a premium, a reward. The product of generosity or, in the reverse, a kind of bribe to encourage harder work or better behavior. In the simplest framework, just a little unanticipated extra.

And that last definition is, I think, what my friends R. and C. intended when they framed their winter letter around the doings of their past "bonus year." Teachers, political operatives, out-there social justice advocates, travelers, R. and C. are 80ish. Grandchildren and medical capers, they wrote, defined their "bonus time." An accompanying Xeroxed photograph featured their current selves with an inset image of the two of them locked in a kiss, forty years earlier.

So I've been puzzling over "bonus years" for a week now.

I'm struck first by the reality that too many good, talented, contributing people never get bonus time. No matter if they "earned" it or simply as an unexpected extra. The most vibrant member of my high school debate team died at 19; Mother's best friend Rachel at 42; Dave at 63; cousin Gary at 73; Ivan Doig at 75. C. lost a wildly creative son in his 30s. Millions of young men and women recruited into military uniforms. And across time, across the world, billions taken early by hunger and massacre. Good lives shortened by diseases that seem random and by human decisions that are incomprehensible. No years added to their lives for exemplary behavior. Contributions and artistry never realized.

Then there's the next reality that when we do live longer—those hours can be tricky, difficult, confusing. More than we want to acknowledge, horrifying. We all think now, especially, of dementia and its cruelty—giving us years when we can no longer contemplate, contribute, care for ourselves. For sure, illness and debility is as human as sailing into this final stretch of life in good health. But for those coping with such trouble—and their families—the years are no bonus. No perk. No premium. Far far worse than a fruitcake tin.

Awarding ourselves bonus years has, I think, another side, another liability. These are not pasted on extras, not somehow "dessert" after our ordinary lives. This is life. However many years we live, they are all part of the trajectory of our corporeal selves. How we live the years beyond—say retirement—is as much a part of our being as our career days, our child-rearing time. If—as is true for many of us—we are not putting our shoulder to the wheels of commerce or any eight-to-five position any longer, we still have living and work to do. For sure the work of "being," of investing what we've learned into contemplation and conversations with those around us. Or, indeed, figuring out how to help children and grandchildren or others—help that we likely had little time to provide earlier. In other words, these years aren't "extra;"

they are part of long curve of many lives.

I suspect that, for much of their hard-living, unconventional lives, R. and C. didn't anticipate being old-old. That pivoting to grandchildren and their needs and successes remains an unexpected chapter. Both gifts and mystery that they didn't truly foresee. That's pretty human too. At 40, even with stellar examples of old age in our lives, it's hard to see ourselves there. And if we engage in such envisioning, we feel the terror of awful illness. Or, we envelop ourselves in some great magical realism and find ourselves hiking into the mountains or basking in an Italian square. I think it is harder for us to imagine "ordinary" days. And yet, for many of us, as for my friends, in the midst of slow changes to hearing, eyesight, joints, we are granted sweet routines, precious ordinariness.

But—ordinary—in this life—is extraordinary. The very fact that we are alive is a gift. I've never gotten over Bill Bryson's quotation in *A Short History of Nearly Everything*:

*Not one of your pertinent ancestors was squashed, devoured, drowned, starved, stranded, stuck fast, untimely wounded, or otherwise deflected from its life's quest of delivering a tiny charge of genetic material to the right partner at the right moment in order to perpetuate the only possible sequence of hereditary combinations that could result — eventually, astoundingly, and all too briefly — in you.*

In that sense, every year of my life—including this one that brought me two new knees—is a bonus. A life that I didn't earn. Furthermore, a life of remarkable security and adventure and love—rare in the panoply of human experience.

Finally, I'm intrigued by R. and C.'s deliberate inclusion of that earlier photo—a glimpse of their younger, passionate selves. If, if we are fortunate enough to arrive at these final years, we often want—desperately—to remember that we were young. To celebrate ourselves when we were beautiful, vibrant, powerful. Memory care units post photos of their residents from many years ago. Obituaries often include young adult images. No matter how much we intellectualize the worth of age, we struggle against a universe that validates youth far more. In spite of ourselves, we long for earlier chapters, earlier adventures, earlier tender moments? In other words, do most of us now, find these years—these bonus years—rather like my father's red tin of fruitcake: a dicey, insufficient reward for the lives we've lived?

March 2024

## Pleasant

A month beyond my second knee replacement surgery, I've had time to consider the bizarre parts of this experience. Including the label I was awarded in doctor's notes. Formulaic, dictated, once considered almost classified, such records are now readily available to patients. And even with medical jargon, useful.

Three separate such reports noted that I'm a "pleasant 77 yr. old." Shit! Really? Not interesting. Or articulate. Or well-read. Or lively. Or cheerful. Not even worried. Or obstreperous. Or whiny.

Just pleasant. Of course, the surgeon dictating this had spent all of four minutes with me prior to the operating room. Of course, he knew that I would read the document—so he was careful not to offend. Maybe he had a list of acceptable adjectives to employ. On the scale of stuff for him to consider, this tiny label holds no real import.

So why do I flinch? Why do I care?

I do intend to be pleasant most of the time. Although this last surgery prep required me to stand my ground against a grizzled, patronizing, just-plain-wrong anesthesiologist. But whether or not I always feel cheerful, I know that pleasantness works far better most of the time than grumpiness. It's the lovely olive oil of human interaction. So, the word itself isn't offensive.

The number also startles me. I know that I'm 77. The medical world uses our birthdates as identification—as proof that they are working on the correct patient. So I must have reiterated my birthdate a dozen times in two days. But when YOU say my age, I'm a little chagrined.

Am I really THAT old? I'm inclined to shout out, "yes, but there are extenuating factors!" or "yes, but my neck isn't as wrinkly as yours."

My revulsion to being characterized as a "pleasant, 77 yr. old" comes, I think, from the composite, the fusion. From the fear that what I have to show for 77 years of living is run-of-the-mill pleasantness. That all my living—all my careers—all my friendships—all my writing—all my passions boil down to a Campbell's soup of living—a can of pleasantness. Is that all that I am?

Still, here at 77 (or for that matter, any age), my task isn't to argue the label so automatically applied by a busy surgeon. But to decide how I want to invest these days. To determine what I can do with two improving knees to savor the world and the amazing experiences I'm offered.

So, what the **#@*, Marcella. Move on to something that matters more than what Dr. Schlepp dictated at the end of a busy day of surgery!

February 2024

## Invalid

Last evening, I took myself off to bed at the usual time—having done some minor tidying around the house. I'd settled in reading when one of the boys began yowling, thumping, scratching, throwing objects around—somewhere. Tiger Tiger appeared right away, but Tuxedo was not in his known hiding places: the washing machine drum, the dishwasher, or any lower cupboard. I was slow to realize that the ruckus came from my tiny pantry. That Tuxedo must have gotten in when I stowed away cereal and cookies. I opened the door frantically—in other words, quickly—to be bowled over by a flying box of graham crackers, leftover Halloween candy, full bottles of Tanqueray gin and Johnnie Walker Red and a topless jar of sesame oil. Which whipped around like a whirling dervish before emptying itself out on the entry rug. Tuxedo had flown out first.

I'm six weeks beyond my left knee replacement surgery. Were it not for the rapid disintegration of my right knee scheduled for replacement early in January, I'd be pretty stable. But not enough to get down on my haunches to begin the degreasing process. I returned briefly to bed—hoping to let the mess go until morning. And then second-guessed myself. I got back up and deployed fistfuls of Lysol wipes—reaching as far as I could from a chair and then affixing the wipes to my ever-handy old-people grabber. I got the rug into a garbage bag and wiped down the bottles that didn't break but got doused. And then returned to bed—with orange, oily feet.

I am not an IN'valid. And haven't been since my surgery. If your imagination runs like mine you picture a wicker wheel chair with a shaky figure clad in a blue robe whose lap and legs are covered by a blanket. Or you see an old lady propped up in bed wearing a lace bed jacket and sipping from one of those Victorian feeding cups—half spout and half bowl. Thanks to "modern" medicine I was out of bed and walking the same day as my surgery. The floor nurse couldn't wait to discharge me the following morning and never offered to help me dress. I came home to thoughtful, wise friends who helped rearrange the house just enough to make navigating with a walker easy. I began physical therapy at a nearby clinic two days later.

Now, I've retired the walkers til January, can do my own laundry, fill and empty the dishwasher, pop cocktail hour popcorn, play fetch with Tuxedo until he's bored. So, I don't feel like an IN'valid.

What I feel keenly is inVAL'id.

The words are, of course, from exactly the same origin: Latin *in-validus*, not-strong. Their more obvious application is, of course, for sick folks. Folks experiencing a long or wasting illness.

But the version that plagues me also means without a strong foundation, something not based in fact, OR no longer useful or current.

Bingo. In many ways, growing into and through these retirement years is all an exercise in inVALidity. An exercise in trying to feel useful and current. To understand a changing world. To feel a bit of prowess after we've outgrown the careers or at least the money-making chapters of our lives. To keep adept enough at our devices to reach children and read the news.

We feel an inVAL'id when we are pandered to, when our white hair or slow walk earns us a hand offered too quickly. Or a sharp reminder that—to someone else—we look unsteady. Even sometimes when we might be grateful for assistance, we blanche when younger folks just assume that we need them. Or need their sharp advice on what we should or shouldn't do. And we really really bridle when our children or grandchildren watch how we park the car or take a left hand turn or slip into our garages. Caring is so often braided with one strand of smugness or impatience.

My further experience of inVAL'idity during these last two months has been the absence of a real foundation: a new, fake knee that's learning its duty and an old one that has outworn its usefulness. And because I've had such good help, such incredibly skilled and thought-ful assistance from friends, I've been able to coddle both knees. And to sink into a kind of decadent and pampered life. Need a snack, "Here, I'll get it for you." "Let me take the trash out." "Here's today's mail." "You can just flip the coffee pot on in the morning."

What a life! Except, of course, my own slide from recovery to lazy. From recommended rehabilitation to not-so-recommended stagna-tion. What an easy, alluring regression it's been. Lovely, except for the slight bite removed from my self-respect. Except for the potent danger of inertia. Which danger runs rife through these years anyway.

I have a "to do" list here by my elbow and have made some head-way today. And this season of Christmas demands action and activity. And once moving—just like our physics teachers taught us—I'll keep moving and feel good about it.

But I suspect that this season of knee replacement is also a good time to remember that we are all—in the end—beings not doings. That our lives are measured in the depth of our joy in our fellow creatures and the world's complexity and beauty. And in our efforts to help and celebrate those creatures and the world. And, when I get to thinking—and moving a bit—there are countless ways to do that without being a young whippersnapper.

The lessons of aging well (or living well) don't quit, do they. How I perceive myself—valid or inVAL'id—remains my choice. Even if or when I become an INvalid in that lacy bed jacket, I can choose to see myself as whole, as a person, as a life, as a spirit. And for sure, as I spend time with contemporaries, I witness what self-possession, self-respect looks like whether or not my friends require "mobility aids."

The morning after the sesame oil disaster, the pump on my boiler quit. I woke to a cold house. Yet another trying moment when hobbling around seemed twice as frustrating, another insult to my independence. But—but—one call to the plumber on whom I've depended for fifteen years not only resulted quickly in a functioning boiler. Todd also gave me latitude to skip the office next time disaster struck and just call him directly. We live in a sea of good hearts who usually take us as we are: INvalid or inVAL'id. Weak or strong or struggling or blooming.

December 2023

## Malaise AND Season of Grace

I know that the tattoo on my arm says "YES YES YES YES YES," but right now I'm feeling "NO NO NO NO NO." In fact, I've spent the last several days trying to construct a clever—not too indulgent or discouraging—essay about this current mood. I even tried to conjure an uplifting thesis and haunted the thesaurus for organizing descriptions: passage, renewal, transformation. When the right theme all along was——malaise.

The condition that led me to leave an assortment of groceries delivered Sunday afternoon still out on my counter top and patronize three fast food businesses in two days. The condition that accounts for why

I do the laundry and then proceed to dress myself from the dryer until I can't. The condition in which I devoted two hours yesterday to watching and listening to my old 70s hip-swiveling idol Tom Jones on YouTube. (PS: His voice is really good and his face is now cherubic—angelic even though—according to Wikipedia—yes another diversion—he screwed more than 250 groupies in a year).

You see what kind of state I'm in. And it's not helped by the 35 mile-per-hour winds we're experiencing to be followed by a night and day of rain and snow. (YEEESSS, I KNOW WE NEED THE MOISTURE!!!) Nor by the "check engine" light (always a fickle indicator of the Matrix's health) that's been on for a week now. Nor by a letter from the Montana Department of Revenue that swears I didn't file my 2022 taxes even though they cashed my check last March 8, 2023.

What's more, there is no logical reason for this bout of disquiet. For god's sake, I have two shiny new functioning knees that were installed with minimum pain. I was spoiled rotten during my surgical recuperation. Rotten—it's not an exaggeration. My physical therapist has become a skilled, wise friend. And when I got a bad case of bronchitis in the aftermath, I was again worried over and lavished with attention. And then, and then, the two kidney stones that made an appearance disappeared nicely when blasted by sound waves in a pretty sweet procedure.

I can breathe easily, bend my knees to pick up cat toys, slide in and out of the shower without risking a fall. And despite today's menacing gloom, I know that we're only six weeks away from the height of summer.

The boys—Tiger Tiger and Tuxedo—grew closer to me and vice versa. We all but talk with each other. More times than not they find a way to be adjacent. Tuxedo drools when I pet him. Tiger Tiger spends more time than ever snuzzling—cuddled up on my chest burrowing into my neck—nose and claws.

So what's up?

I wish that I didn't have to name it, but the answer likely revolves around age. The constellation of too much time to think this winter; too many obits for contemporaries; too many hours waiting in the ophthalmologist's office on macular degeneration injection day; too many younger friends dealing with life-threatening illnesses. Perhaps my denial of a couple other small physical annoyances—a twinge of carpal tunnel, for instance. Maybe even too many obstacles quietly cleared from my path—no snow shoveling, coffee made for mornings, the trash spirited away.

Likely yet another instance in which my protestations about growing older and dying being an ordinary part of life are more bravado than candor. There have been moments this winter when, perhaps courtesy of good drugs, I felt easy about drifting off. Where sweet quiet, sweet sleep felt so good. Where—for a time—the need for adventure or some gadget from Amazon fell away. Where—so long as more fine books waited for me on Kindle, so long as my supply of Lemon Oreos and Pepperidge Farm Milanos held, so long as I could snuggle under this new generation of impossibly fleecy blankets—I wanted nothing else. Just comfort.

But this malaise tells me something else, too. It isn't really that I want to let go into eternity. I do love so much of the life I'm living. In fact, these cobalt-chromium knees offer new destinations. Just not an eternal one. That—I think—is the malaise-inducing conundrum. I can do more than I did a year ago, but not roll back the years I've lived. Which means, in all honesty, I need to be real-pragmatic-practical. And more than ever live what's livable.

I know only to start by tackling the obvious chores that are literally strewn around me. Getting to YES by saying yes to some activity and accomplishment. Then maybe stepping away from philosophizing about death. Instead to take it in—really really. To move to a slightly different place—a different plateau. To quit flinching when I say 77. To quit flinching as I look at my comrades waiting for macular degeneration shots. To find a way to savor without squeezing experiences to death—literally. To get my years-old gratitude journal out and put it front and center on my desk.

And then, I think, I better find the existential rubber band that's held me together for these 77 years. The playing-safe-one. The doing-the-right thing one. The living-on-everything-but-the edge one. And give it up. Give it the hell up.

~ ~ ~

Shirley Robinett's the master of delicate, magical collage. Artistry borne of her tender, observant heart and eyes and the earth's simplest ingredients: recycled paper, feathers, salt, grass, leaves, flowers, seeds, paint. I stumbled into Shirley's greeting cards—amazingly clear photographs of her original collages. And had purchased enough to receive her emails. So I had the opportunity to catch the sale of a simple, powerful original in which Shirley layered the trunks of aspen with a few branches and in them settled two chickadees.

She titled it "Season of Grace."

Which seemed destined for my walls. And names what I want this time in my life to be. Both slow-to-emerge spring. And these years. Maybe to give up that existential noose not with violence but to absorb, to lean into, to concentrate on once again this dazzling land that surrounds me, the friends and cats and family who hold me close, the words and stories on which I feed. Song and shelter and loveliness. Grace.

May 2024

## So the Question of How to Age...

### Begins with assuming:

No special privileges

No certainty of infirmity

No guaranteed treatment

Neither limits nor the absence of limits.

And believing:

Only that every day is the only day

Only that every day, every task, every trouble, every meeting is a gift.

That I am capable of doing more

Or something else in a new way.

That my heart is capable of being bigger, softer,

That I can be an improving friend,

Savvy about the workings of the world.

That I can push myself to eat better, walk more, think more carefully;

That I can try new things and learn, over and over, the exhilaration of trying.

That I can make a dent in the fear, anxiety, self-centeredness—the fences of my construction.

That I will address the need in front of me as much as I look to some "out there" good I could do.

That I will live only in gratitude.

March 2023

*I wrote this page of thoughts on a Sunday morning, July 25, 2010—more than a dozen years ago. Winter's sorting brought it back to my attention. And I find it more relevant now than ever. More timely. More undone. More unlived.*

## When I Grow Too Old to Dream

*We have been gay, going our way*
*Life has been beautiful, we have*
*been young*
*After you've gone, life will go on*
*Like an old song we have sung*

*When I grow too old to dream*
*I'll have you to remember*
*When I grow too old to dream*
*Your love will live in my heart*

*So, kiss me my sweet*
*And so let us part*

*And when I grow too old to dream*
*That kiss will live in my heart*

*And when I grow too old to dream*
*That kiss will live in my heart*

*So, kiss me my sweet*
*And so let us part*
*And when I grow too old to dream*
*That kiss will live in my heart.*

The song was born in 1934—at the height of Mother's vibrant, independent life. It held all the magic that Sigmund Romberg could entwine in its notes and all the longing that Oscar Hammerstein could suffuse in its lyrics. A simple poem that made me want to cry every time Mother sang it. Before I could say or spell "poignant." I did not want Mother to grow old. I did not want her to stop dreaming.

Our lives were rich in music. At church, a huge pipe organ, choirs, a grand piano, and a congregation capable of singing four-part harmony unaccompanied. At home, my folks often slid their classical 78s onto our Stromberg Carlson record player. The hinged piano stool held sheet music for "When I Grow Too Old" and other ballads from Mother's bachelorette days. When trips got long, we sang in the car: She'll Be Coming Round the Mountain; Old Black Joe; Day is Dying in the West.

But Mother sang When I Grow Too Old to Dream largely to herself or to Sonja and me. She intended, I know, to assure us of her love for us, of our preciousness—that we would be her last memories. But the song seemed also to hold Mother's history—much like her unopened trunk stored in our windowless basement backroom. Mementoes of Mother's travel-rich teaching years. Maybe keepsakes of others she had loved.

Mother is gone almost thirty years. I'm conscious of the questions that I never asked her. Of the likelihood that there were chapters in her life that she had little opportunity or freedom to share. I visit again the grief I felt when—having lost her sight—she began to lose her bearings and her ability to speak. I hope so very much that then she could remember our love, our kisses, our hugs—all of them—even the ones we gave so stingily in our teens. And the earlier memories—the ones that predated us. The ones she sang about.

I am a decade younger than Mother when she died. But I am an "old" that surely does not dream grand adventures or loves or accomplishments. Or when I do, I edit them with the realities of wonky hearing and uncooperative knees. Modest dreams. It's a provocative and complicated "old." Many of the companions and icons who I've treasured are gone. And be it measured by knees or ears or obituaries, I live in the limbo, the far fields of my time on earth.

In fact, I am at a place in my life where—as in these essays—remembering becomes joyful and soothing and intriguing. Anchored in powerful friendships, incredible opportunities, travel, work that I held sacred, a family that surrounds me still, beauty, a passion for words.

And, yes, I think about and grieve a bit for what my own future will not hold. And what it will. As I think Mother did. For the "lasts." For the steady and wise surrender of belongings and bonds that we cannot take with us. And for the "firsts" that will not come again—the disbeliefs and joy that blew me back when I stepped off the plane onto European soil; or felt the dark and fraught power of Arlington Cemetery at night or the unfathomable breadth and color of the Grand Canyon. Or Montana skies.

And still, as Mother sang, I revel in the memories that are the bread and wine of my life, the communion with this incredible universe.

*February 2023*

## More–More

Six weeks ago I "enjoyed" a bout of malaise—ultimately tamed by art that spoke of grace, of acceptance. I was fresh off a winter of recovering from knee surgery—and for good measure—kidney stones and bronchitis. I'd been sedentary, reclusive, flat-out waited on. My recovering knees felt like they were held together by thick rubber bands. My walls, even with their art, had become the outer limits of my world rather than our big sky. Those eight sequestered months served their purpose. But took a toll.

It's summer now. My porch geraniums and tomatoes thrive. My annual June visitors—John and Linda—have come and gone. I haven't worn socks for a couple weeks. The windows are open. It's root beer float season. My knees allow me to pick up cat toys off the floor. What more could I want? Especially since I crave these days all the rest of the year.

So, now on the far side of my cloistered life—I want to live. More. Larger. More fully. To move from placidity to purpose. To get the hell off my duff and DO. To end and begin days thinking about more than keeping myself contented with good books and cookies. (I wish that I were employing literary license here, but I'm not.)

This isn't, of course, a revolutionary wish. There are dozens of quotations from luminaries exhorting us to LIVE. To wear purple. To go anything but gently into that good night. To answer Mary Oliver's query, "*. . . what is it you plan to do with your one wild and precious life?*" And time, after all, in my wild and precious life, is whizzing by.

*If not now, when!*

But, as I finish another chapter in yet another good book, I struggle with just what living LARGE means for me—now. In 2024, at this age. Of course just thinking about what I MIGHT do, is not DOING. It's not getting my buns out of the recliner.

I began—a couple days ago—by making a list:

- Invite people over more often.
- Go to more programs and movies.
- Cook a little—especially things I can feed other people.
- Try moving back to bed—rather than settling in to this odd recliner arrangement. [It's a long story that began when I had bronchitis.]
- Walk. Walk. Walk.
- Practice climbing stairs.
- Eat fruit and vegetables.
- Listen to music.
- Go for weeks at a time without buying anything but food— even at thrift stores.
- Play the piano.
- Write. Write. Write—even drivel. Even if I have to rely on writing prompts.
- Take off in the car—see Montana.
- Sit on the porch, close my eyes, and take in the world.
- Write cards and emails and letters every day.
- SEE specifics in daily life that will make outgoing correspondence interesting.
- Play around with collage—my only real craft.
- Flesh out the items on this list.

I let this list simmer for a few days and even acted on a couple of the bulleted items. It didn't much help. I felt all the old, familiar constraints, resistances, laziness. I indulged in my shopworn, disheartening bargaining: "OK, I'll write these three thank-you notes and then I can hurry back to my book and chair."

The list and my skimpy response held no power or freedom. I wasn't living larger. I was still existing within "shoulds." Still keeping the familiar and the easy within reach.

Then I tried to think of more noble projects. MAKE A REAL DIFFERENCE projects. What about sponsoring a child in a foreign country. Biting the bullet and making phone calls for one of the candidates I favor. For sure committing to a decent volunteer position again.

I fumbled around with that idea for a couple more days—knowing—at some subterranean level—that I'd be slow to take on anything big.

Next I summoned advice from the self-help books I'd bought and wrapped myself around hungrily in the 90s. Seeking then—as now—for just the right formula, just the right incantation to live better: *Be in the now. Be present. Focus. Feel the fear and do it anyway. I am good enough. I am beautiful, inside and out. I am exactly where I need to be. My voice is powerful. I embrace the wisdom that comes with each passing year.*

Yikes! None of those admonitions was wrong. They just didn't amount to Bibbity Bobbity Boo. For sure, then as now, it's midnight and I'm still me. I have not been instantly transformed into a more expansive soul.

Finally, finally, when I got quiet enough inside and out, I got closer to diagnosing what keeps me caught in a careful existence: the growing up messages to not stand out, to be a good girl, to be careful, to not risk a leg or a heart or all my money. And to those messages, I've added ones related to age: will it be dark when I drive home; is there a bathroom close by; will I be able to hear; how silly and impossibly old will I look;

how tired will I be.  And maybe the most insidious of all: you're old; you're entitled to rest; you've put in your time; likely there's tomorrow.

What a lot of fear-mongers and killjoys those voices are! Once again, not altogether wrong. Just not helpful.

It took another few days of discontent before I looked at my arm.  And considered why and when I'd gotten three different tattoos. I'd chosen them all in moments when I was hopeful, expansive, living beyond the rules. Every time I'd selected new words for my arm, I'd done so—not for shock value, not on a whim—but as a vow, a declaration to myself about how I intended to live. They were meant to be powerful reminders to live life to the limit. To live the kind of days and emotions that I sought now.

Rather than taking them for granted now, I needed to "hear" in them again what I heard the first time:  possibility, joy, vigor, purpose.  The very moods in which I'd scoped out local tattoo artists and walked through their doors:

**Yes, Yes, Yes, Yes, Yes**
**Still Learning How to Fly**
**Don't Stop Me Now**

Reliving the hours when I decided to add these words permanently to my body, I felt more whole, more alive.  I could summon again the consciousness, the excitement, the possibilities that surround living large—as I had intended then.

**Yes, Yes**—as opposed to no or maybe. **Yes**—as opposed to despair.

**Learning and Flying**—being curious, asking for more information, asking big questions,  taking off into circumstances and places unknown, heading out into uncertainty.

And going on, however I can—**not stopping at all**. Floating in ecstasy, defying the laws of gravity, having such a good time.

I still need that first list of activities for the moments I'm at loose ends.

When I need to be reminded of projects that will contribute to the world, that will bring me satisfaction. Those projects and tasks are likely the warp and woof of living larger.

But in the end, I experience emotional courage and liveliness and wonder less from a checklist and more from remembered joy and purpose. From breathtakingly bigger emotions. From an inestimable awareness that life, that the universe is enormous, flyable, exquisite! And that I am beyond fortunate to be alive in it.

**July 2024**

# CLOSING

## So Damned Lucky - - - And Thankful

Sometime in the winter of 2016, Facebook dropped an invitation onto my screen for a summer "salon" called "Revelations in the Art of Memoir" to be held on the Greek Island of Patmos. It was to be led by Mary Karr and Rodney Crowell. Mostly my racing heart shrieked "RODNEY CROWELL" and I applied on the spot. Turns out the critical qualifications to participate were enthusiasm and enough money for ten days of sun and the sorcery of thoughtful hosts and all the savvy that Rodney and Mary could share. My life spun open on that island.

I came away knowing that—for sure—I didn't have a true memoir to produce. I'd experienced ripples in my life but not the arc of a plotline that books demanded. But surrounded by new deep, powerful friendships—compatriots in creativity and caring—I came home wanting to write and believing that I could.

And here in my 70s, I've been fortunate to have the time and means to natter away on essays of memory and opinion. Still encouraged by longstanding and new friends.

I'm also extraordinarily lucky to have been born to Paul and Esther Sherfy in the lovely little Kansas town of McPherson. To attend good schools and a rational church, head on to college and graduate school, find interesting, meaning-rich work along the way, live on the East Coast and then Montana, marry a fine and fascinating man and relish my role as stepmom.

I have not gone hungry or had to sleep on a sidewalk. I have not been abused or raped. I have not fought through floods or tornadoes or earthquakes or fires. More phenomenal good luck—not granted to most of the humans who've arrived on this earth. I have not "earned" that good fortune. Nor done anything that made me more deserving than every other person.

Especially, I have been surrounded by great companions: all those classmates and teachers in eighteen years of study; all the staff and patrons at the McPherson Public Library; the Alliance Insurance Company "girls;" Gettysburg rangers; D. C. colleagues; an enormous chorus of Montanans who've stood on our historic preservation battle lines for years. A company of incredible friends who entered my life quite by astounding accident.

And so I've fashioned my writing on all that good fortune and the people and places I've known. And that's who and what I want to acknowledge here at the end of this collection. I remain especially grateful to my Patmos brothers and sisters, to Chris Sowers, to Rebecca Stanfel, to Martha Kohl. To the friends—you—near and far who fill my life with laughter and insight and comfort. I write from the bedrock you all provide. And from the sheer wonder of an unusually magical existence. With great thanks! So damned lucky!

*Marcella*